THIS COLORING BOOK BELONGS TO:

....

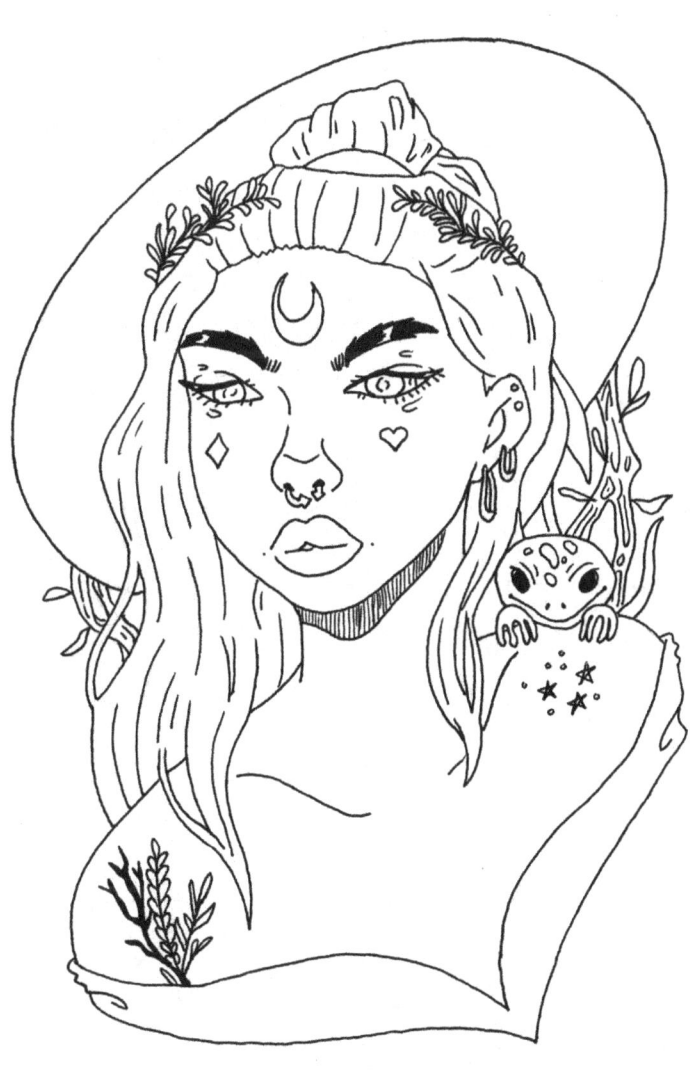

Copyright©2021 Tiskyd Publishing
All rights Reserved

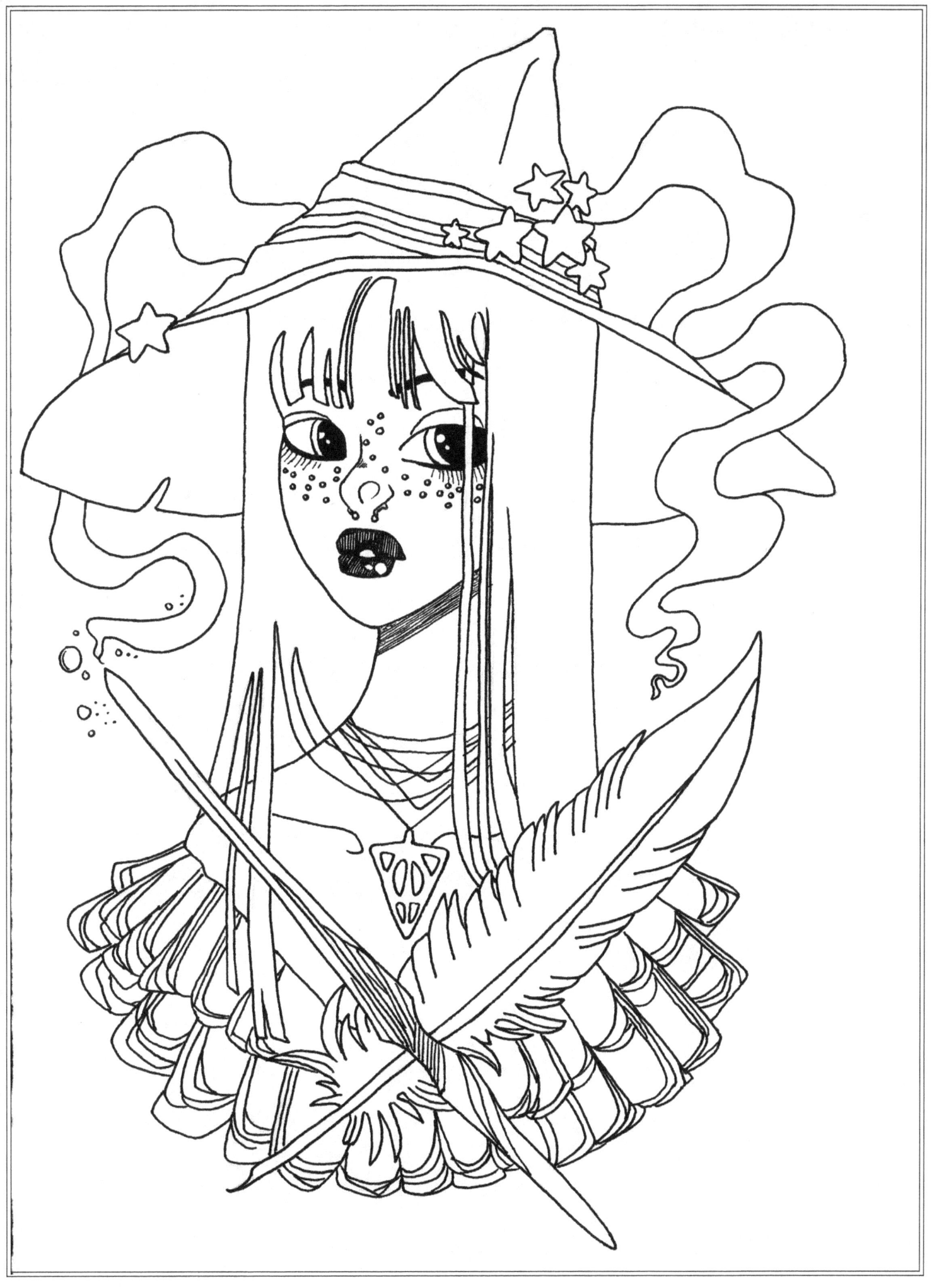

TISKYD Publishing

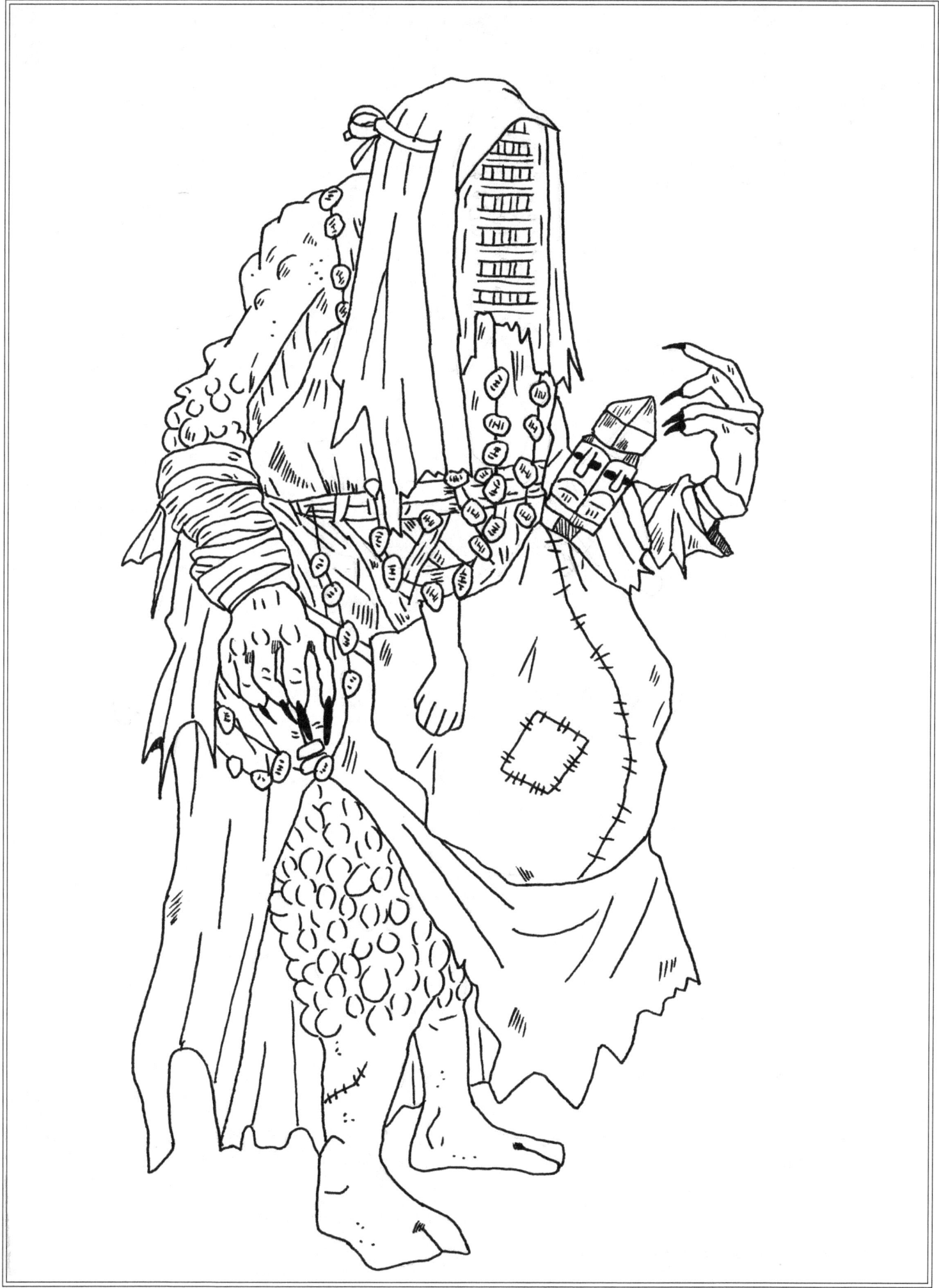

TISKYD Publishing

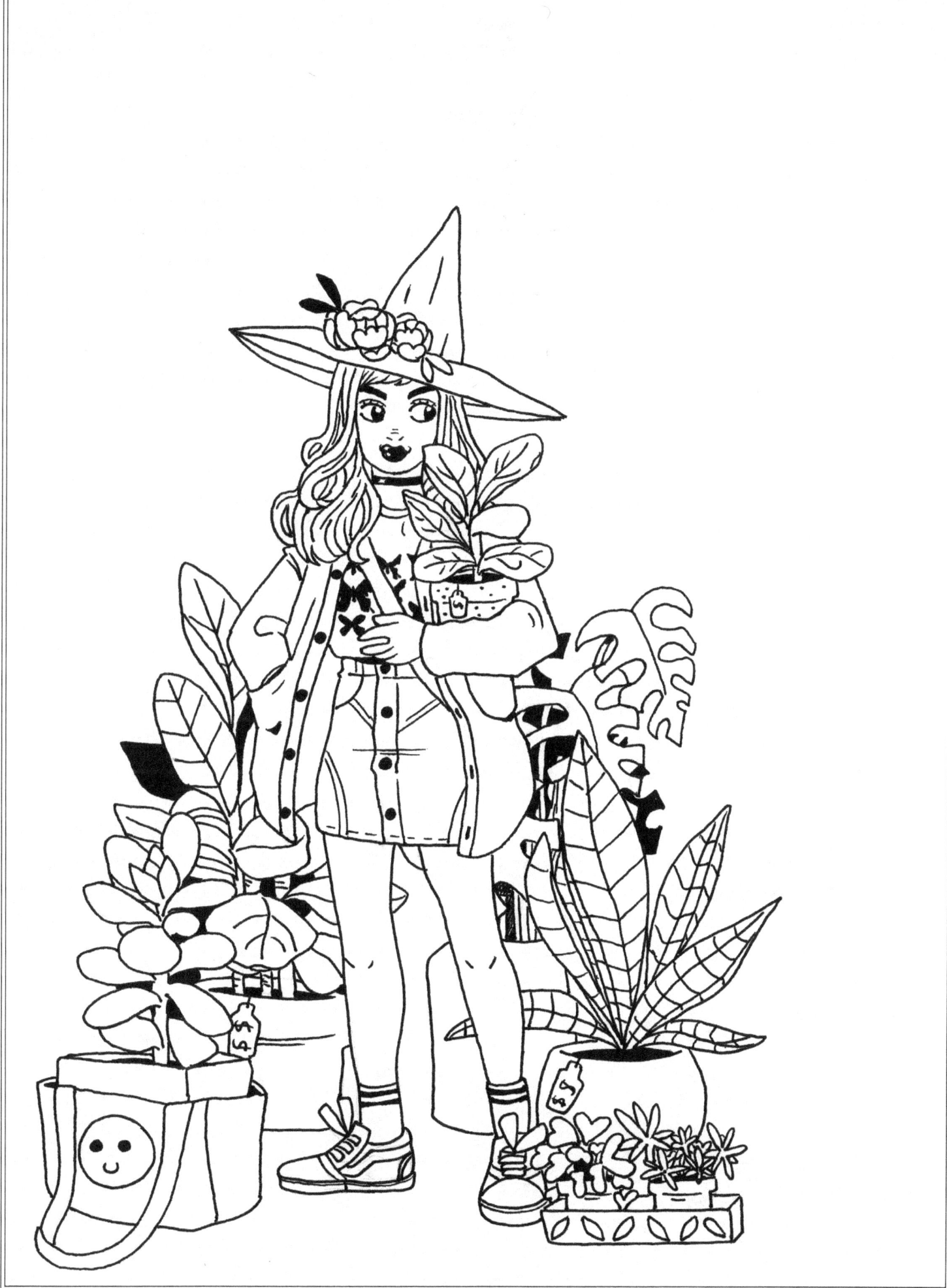

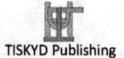

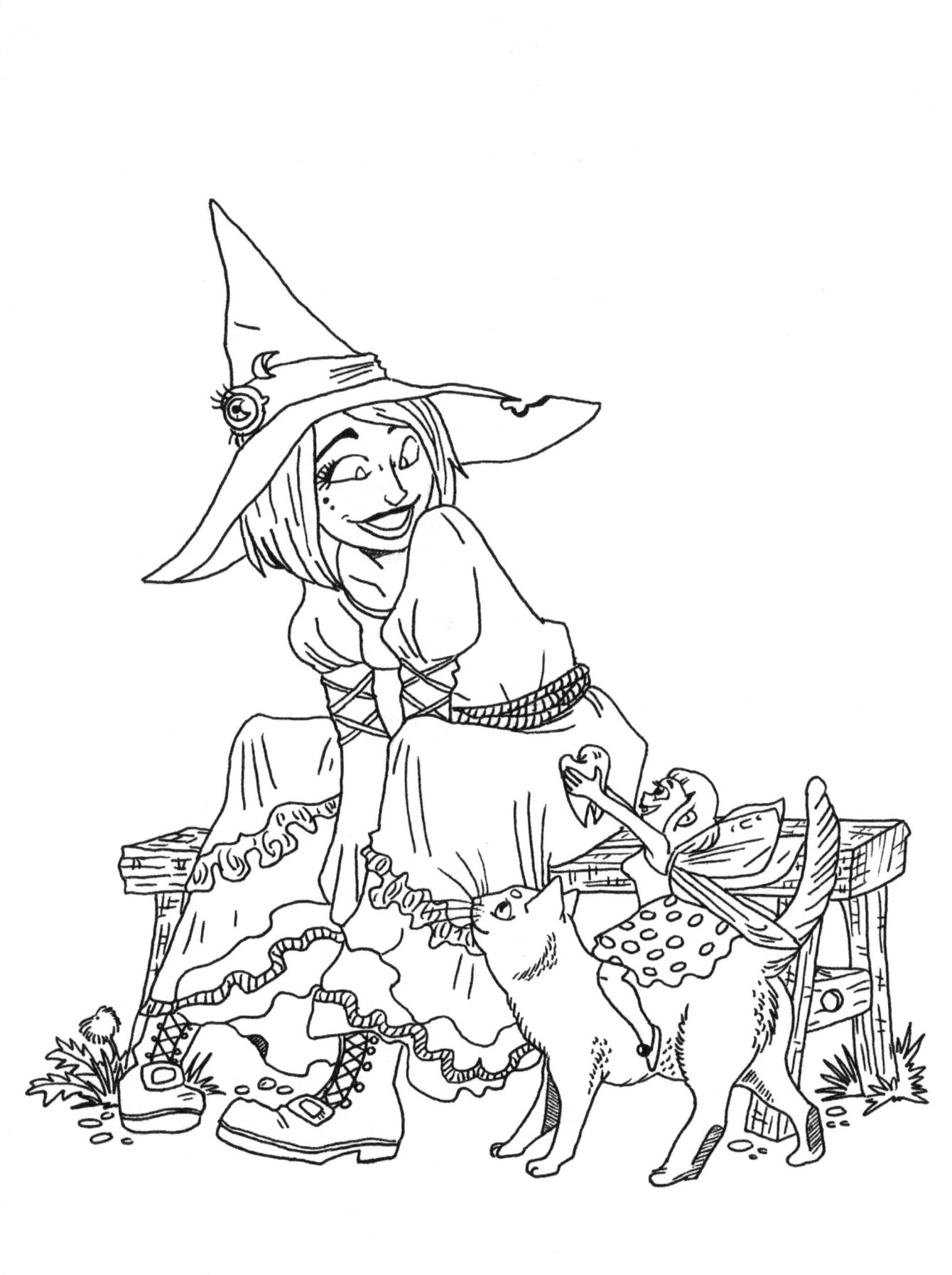

TISKYD Publishing

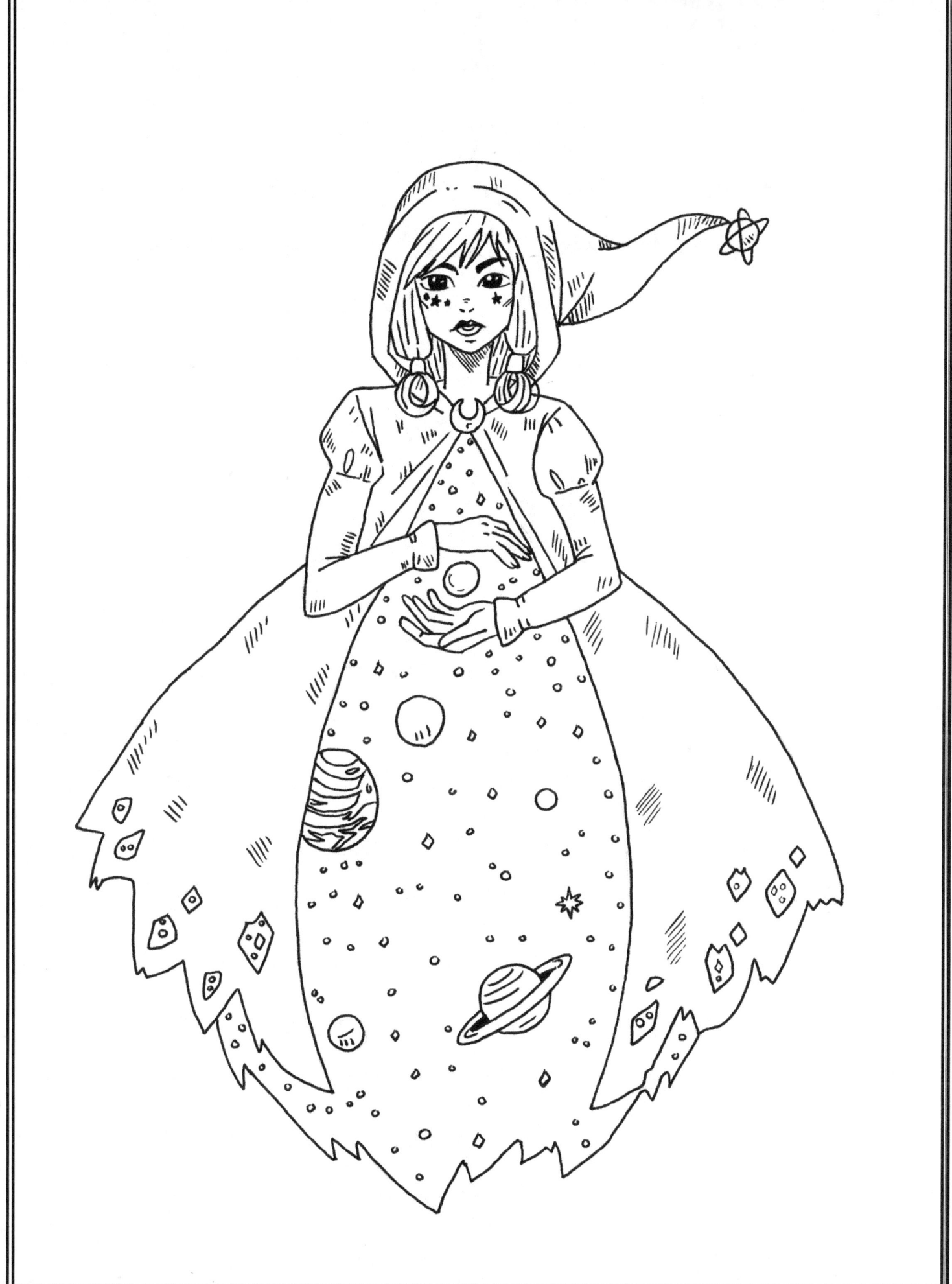

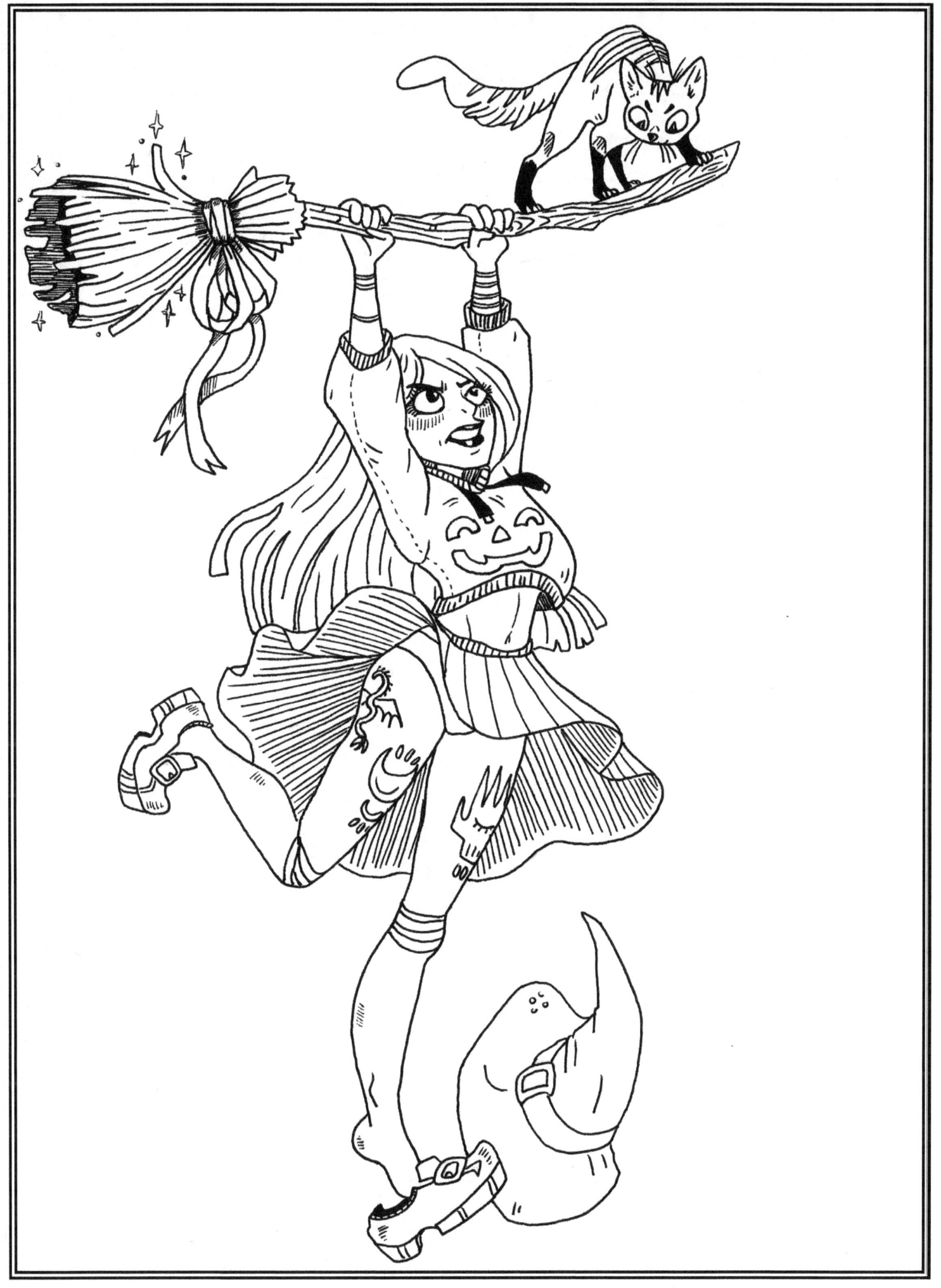

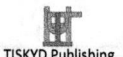

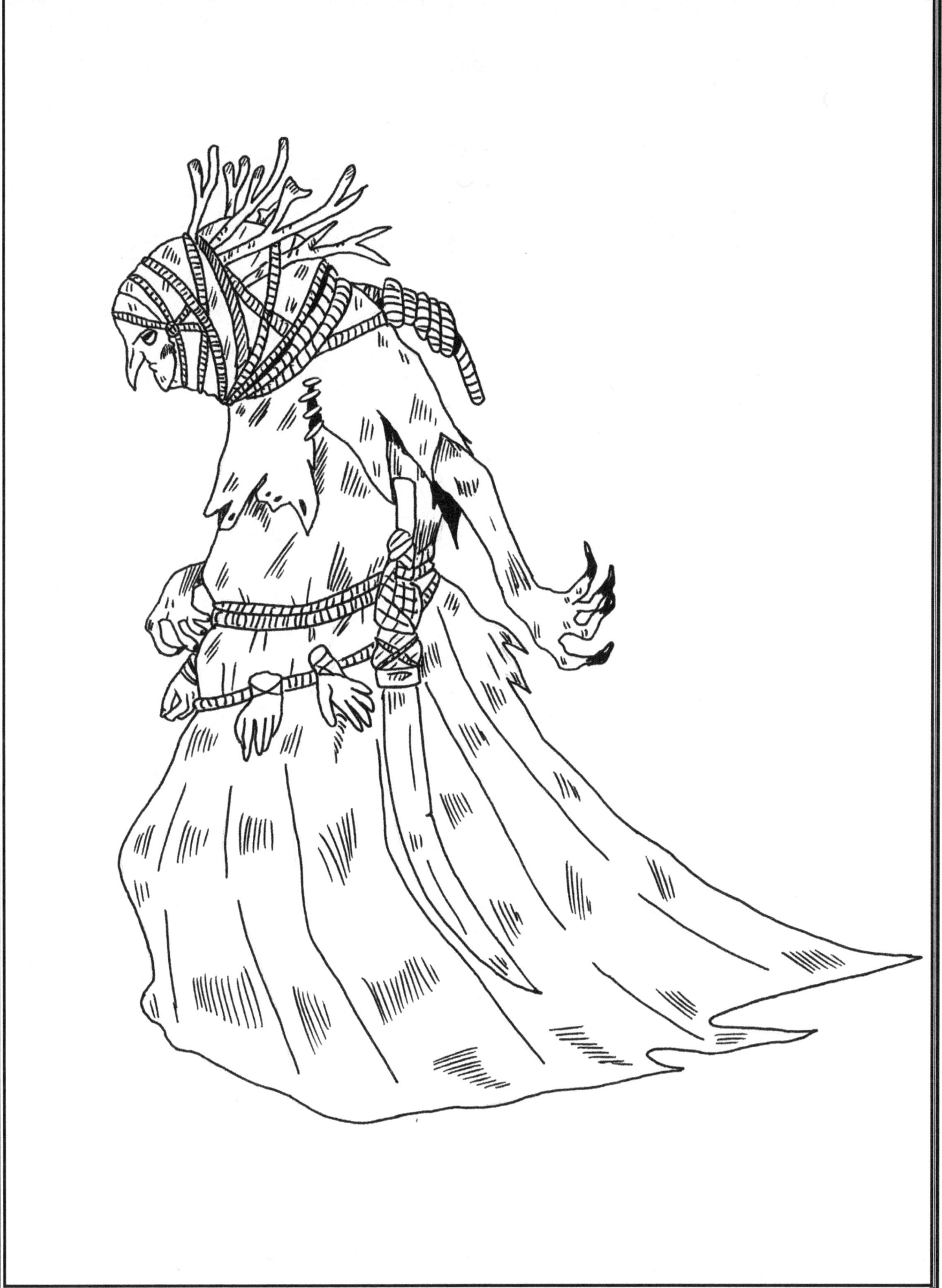

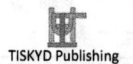

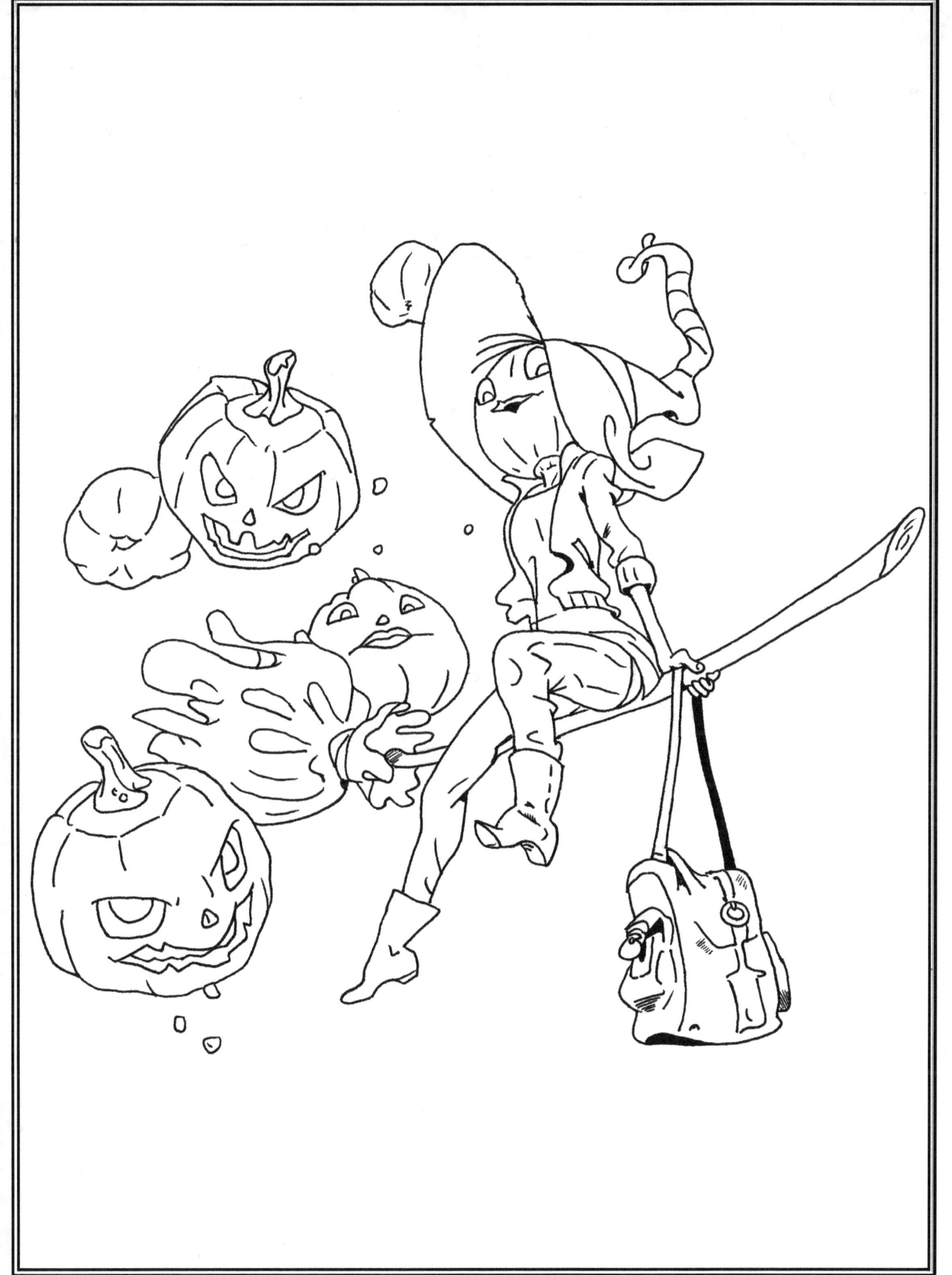

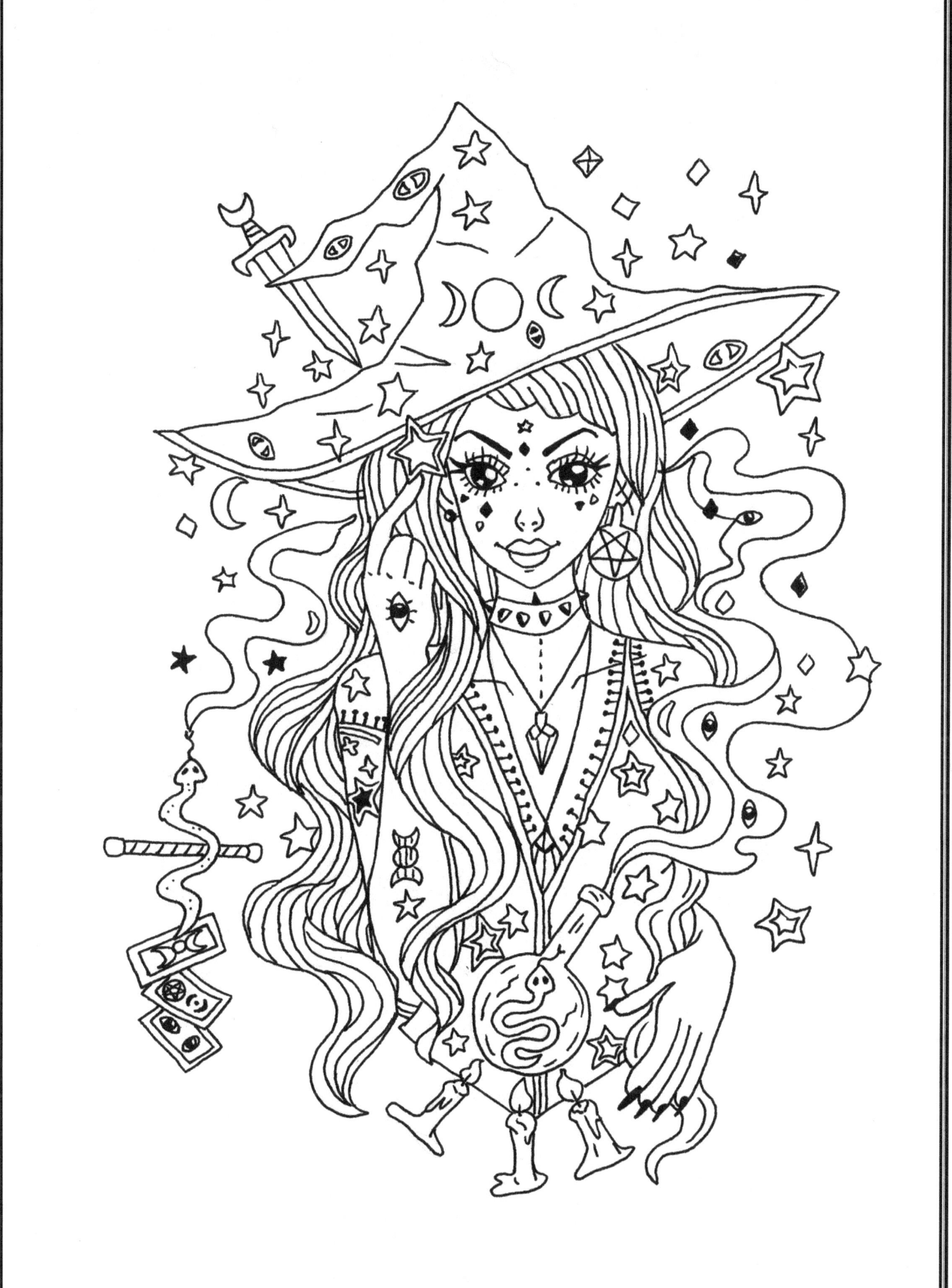

TISKYD Publishing

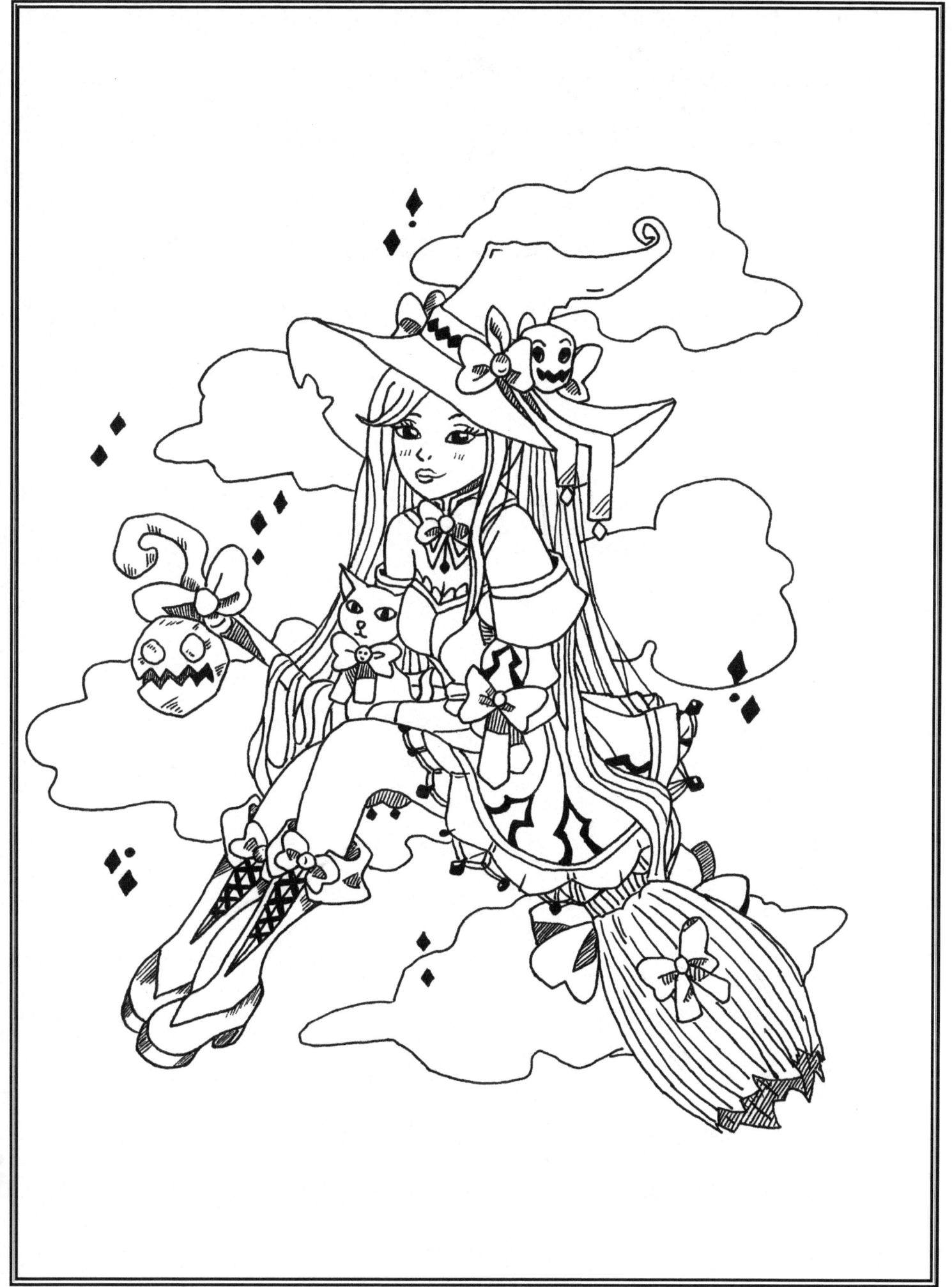

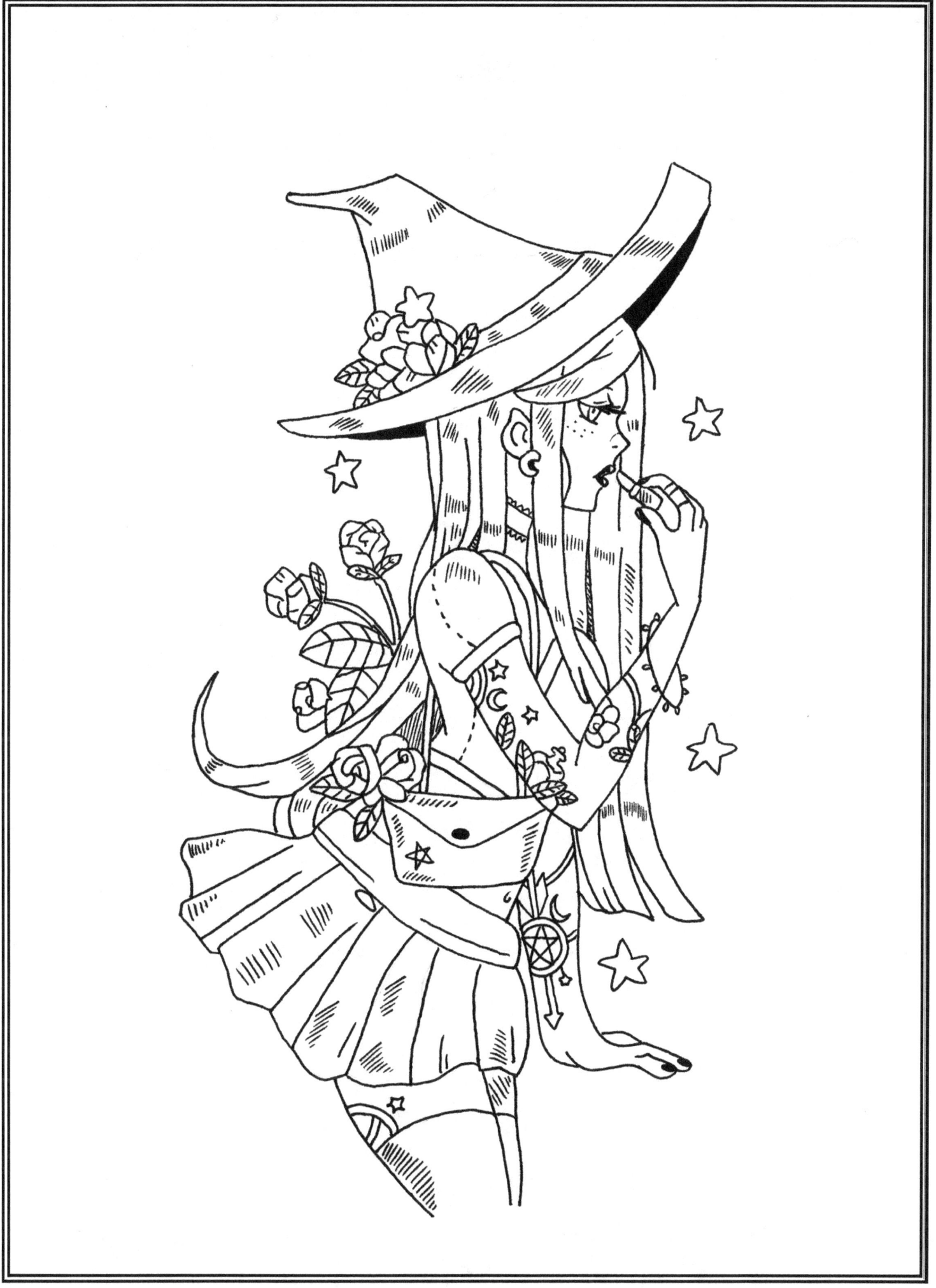

TISKYD Publishing

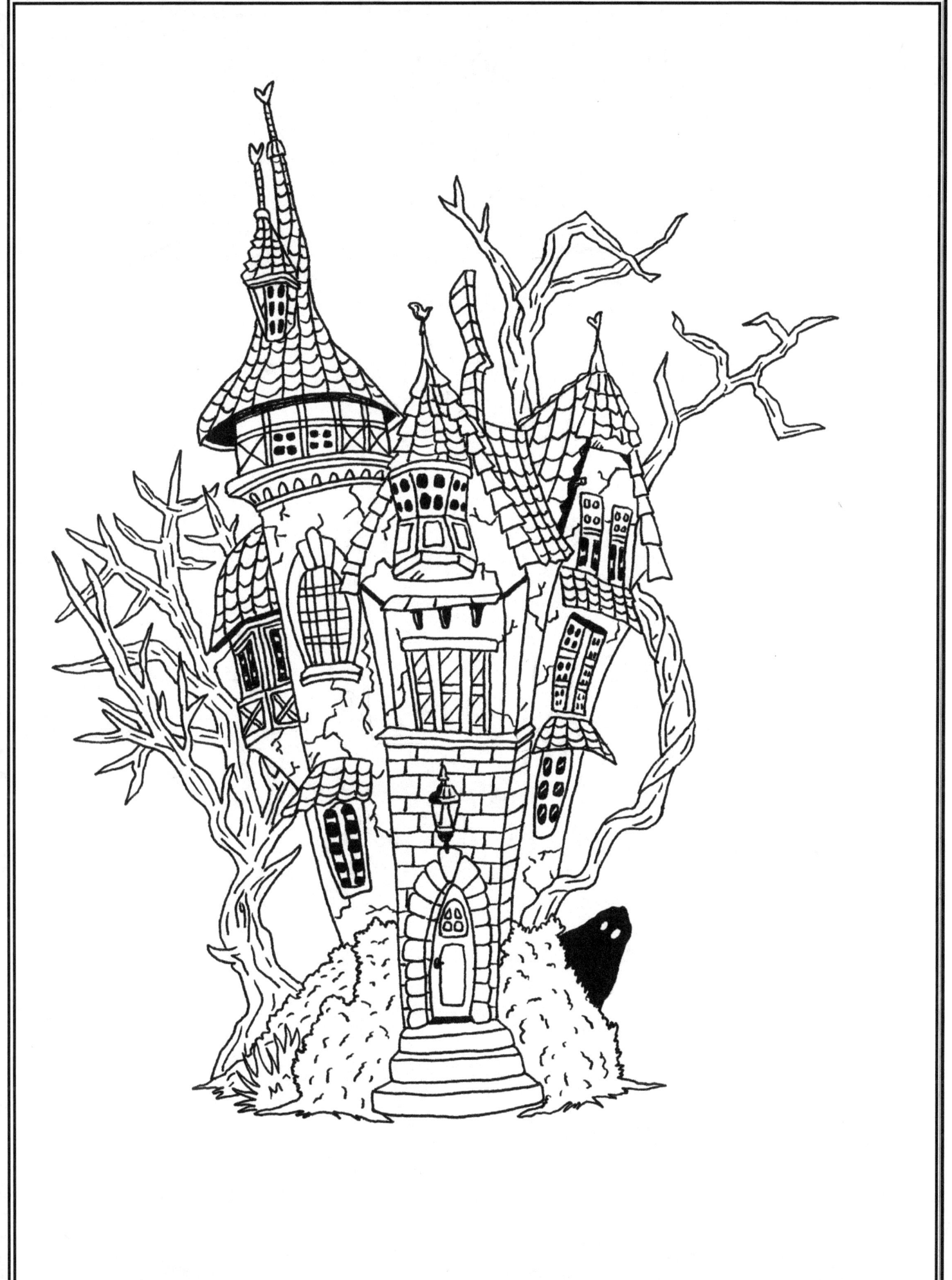

TISKYD Publishing

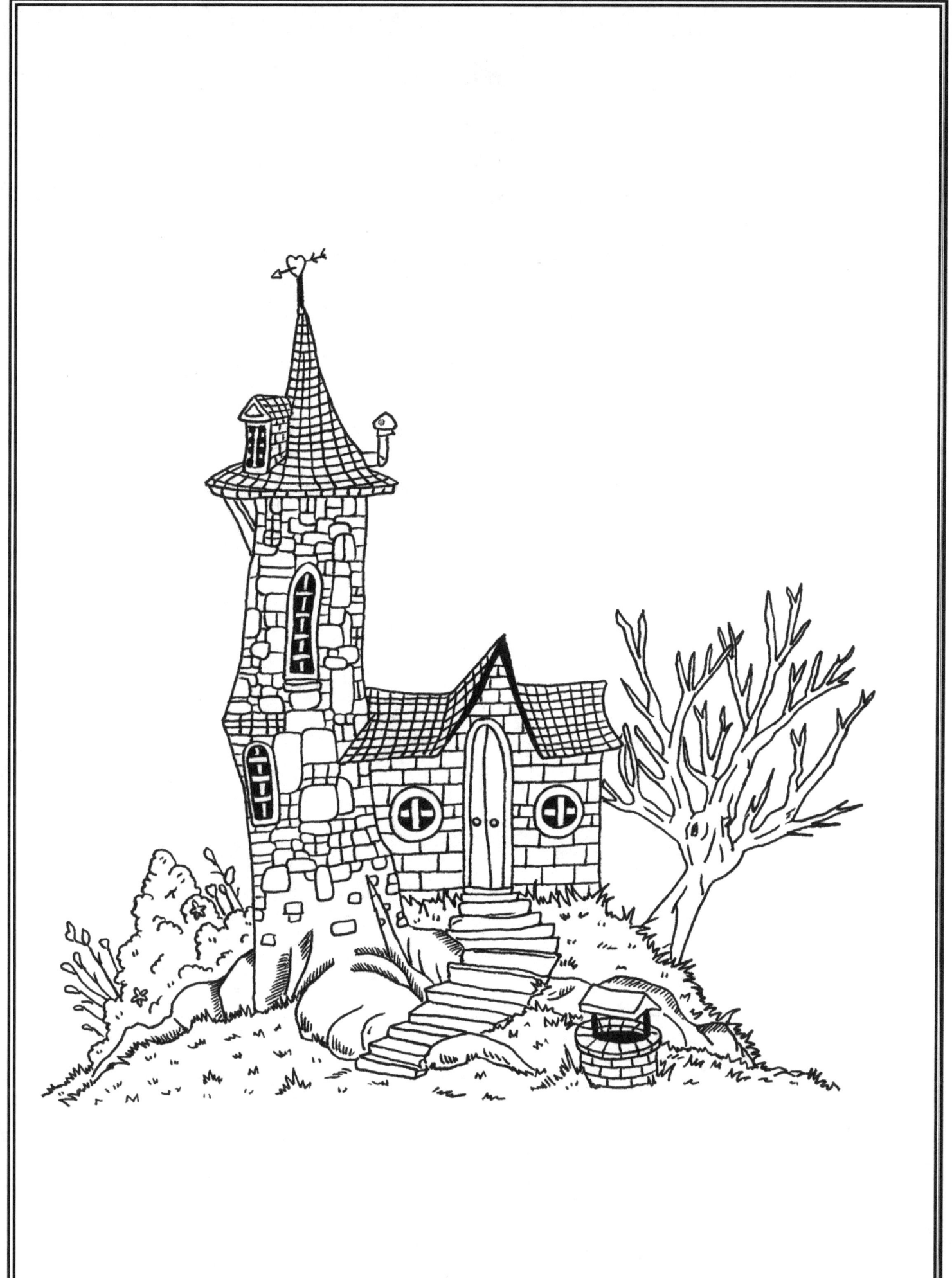

TISKYD Publishing

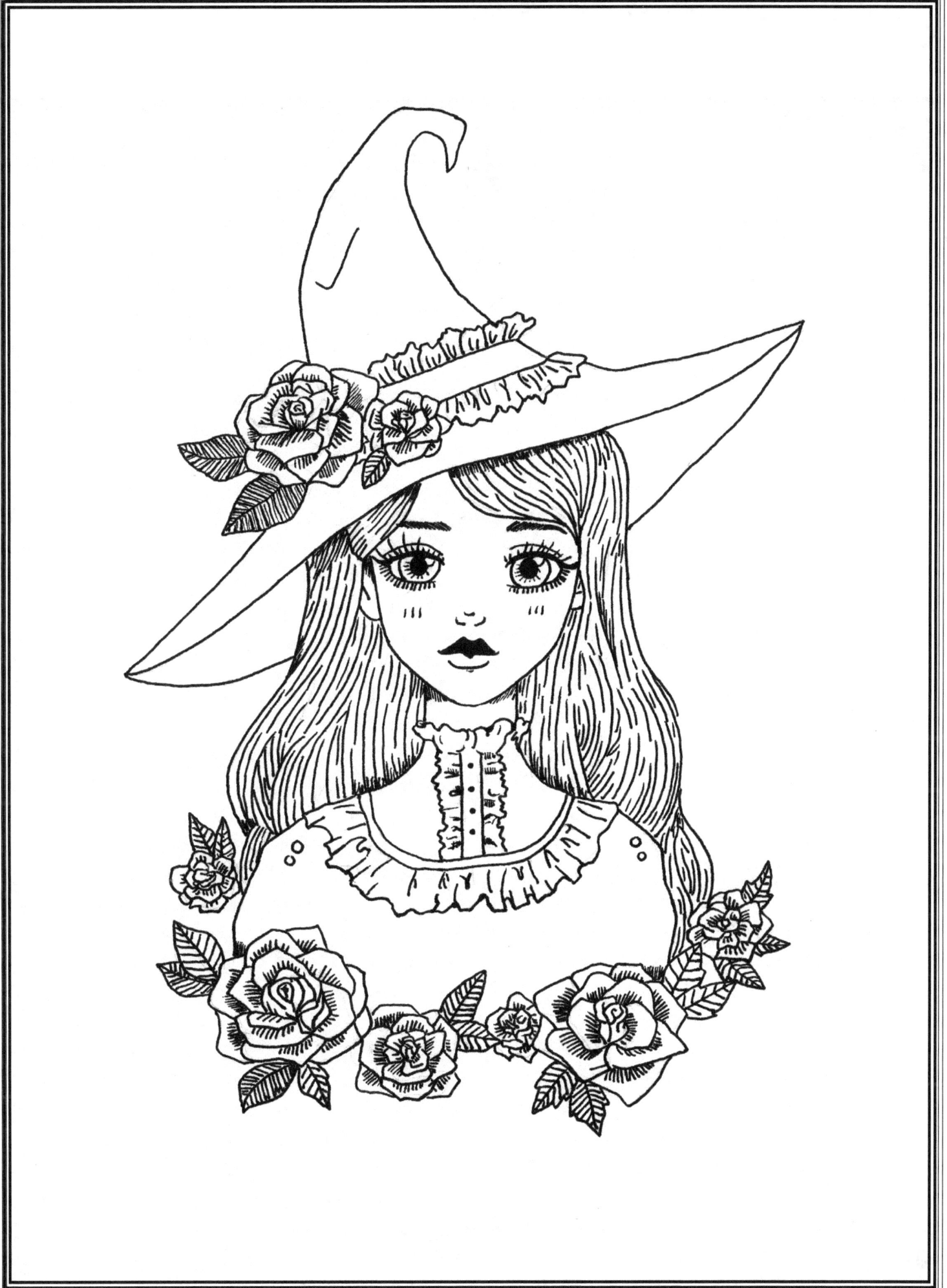

TISKYD Publishing

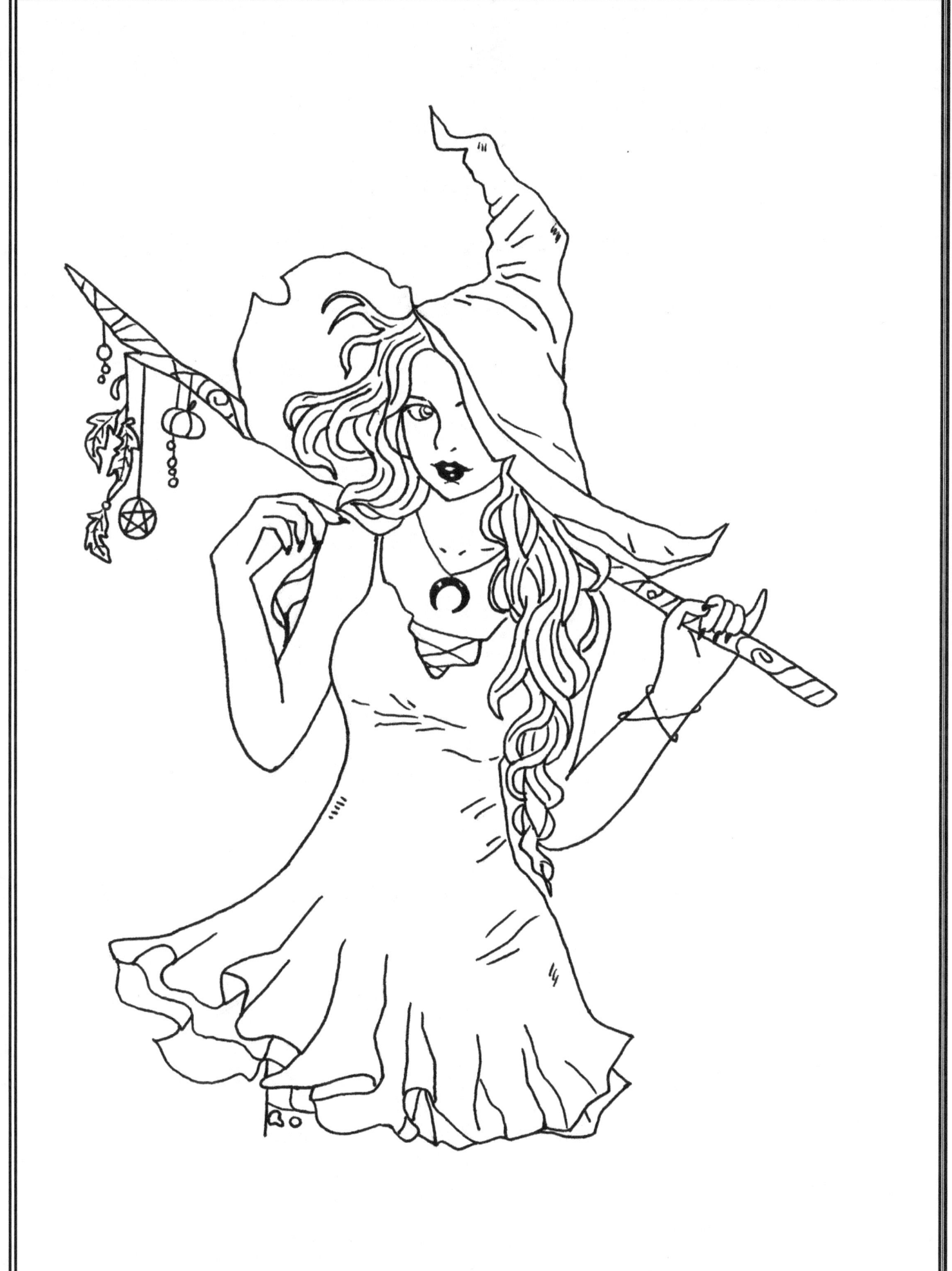

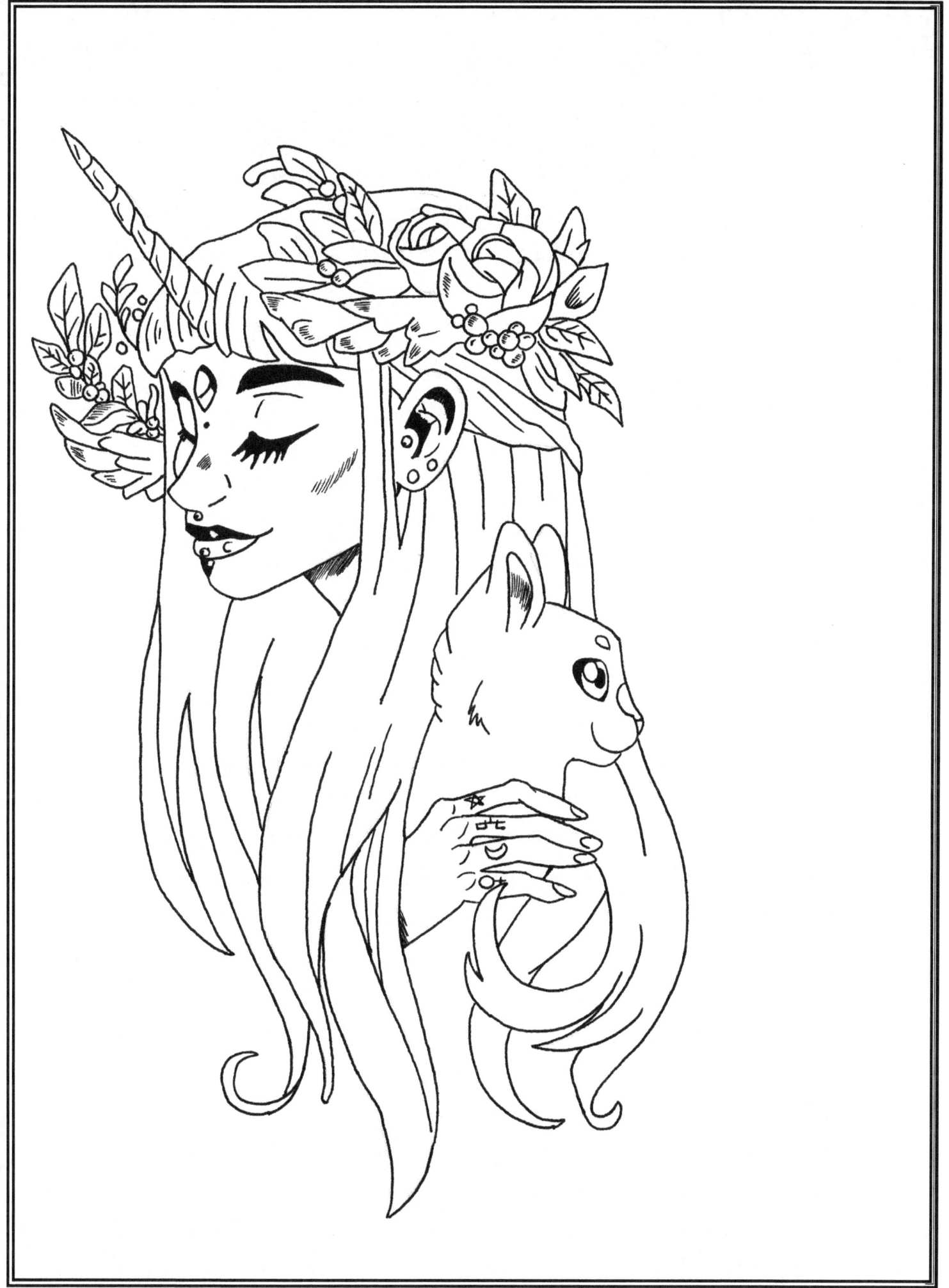

TISKYD Publishing

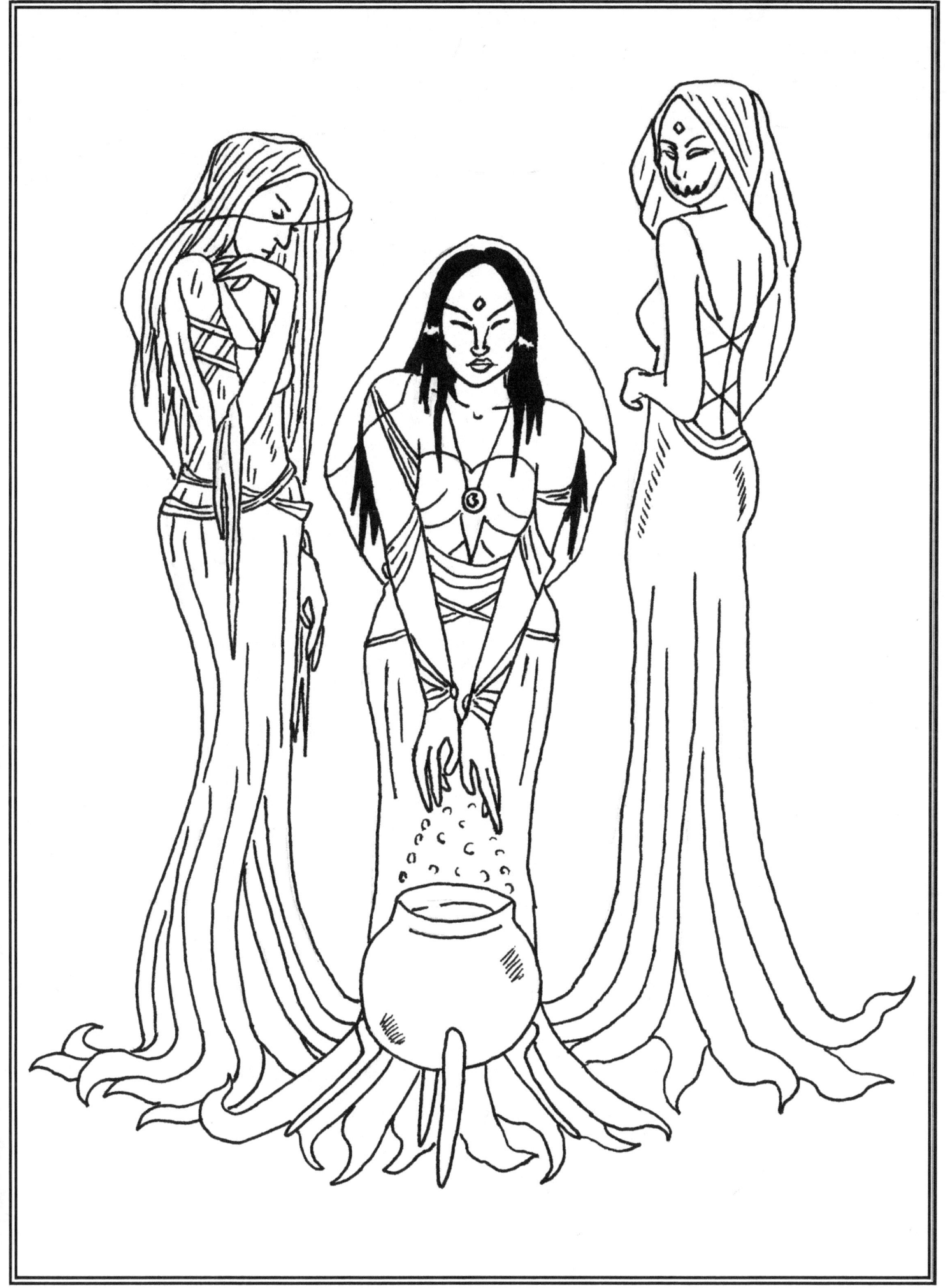

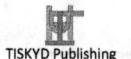
TISKYD Publishing

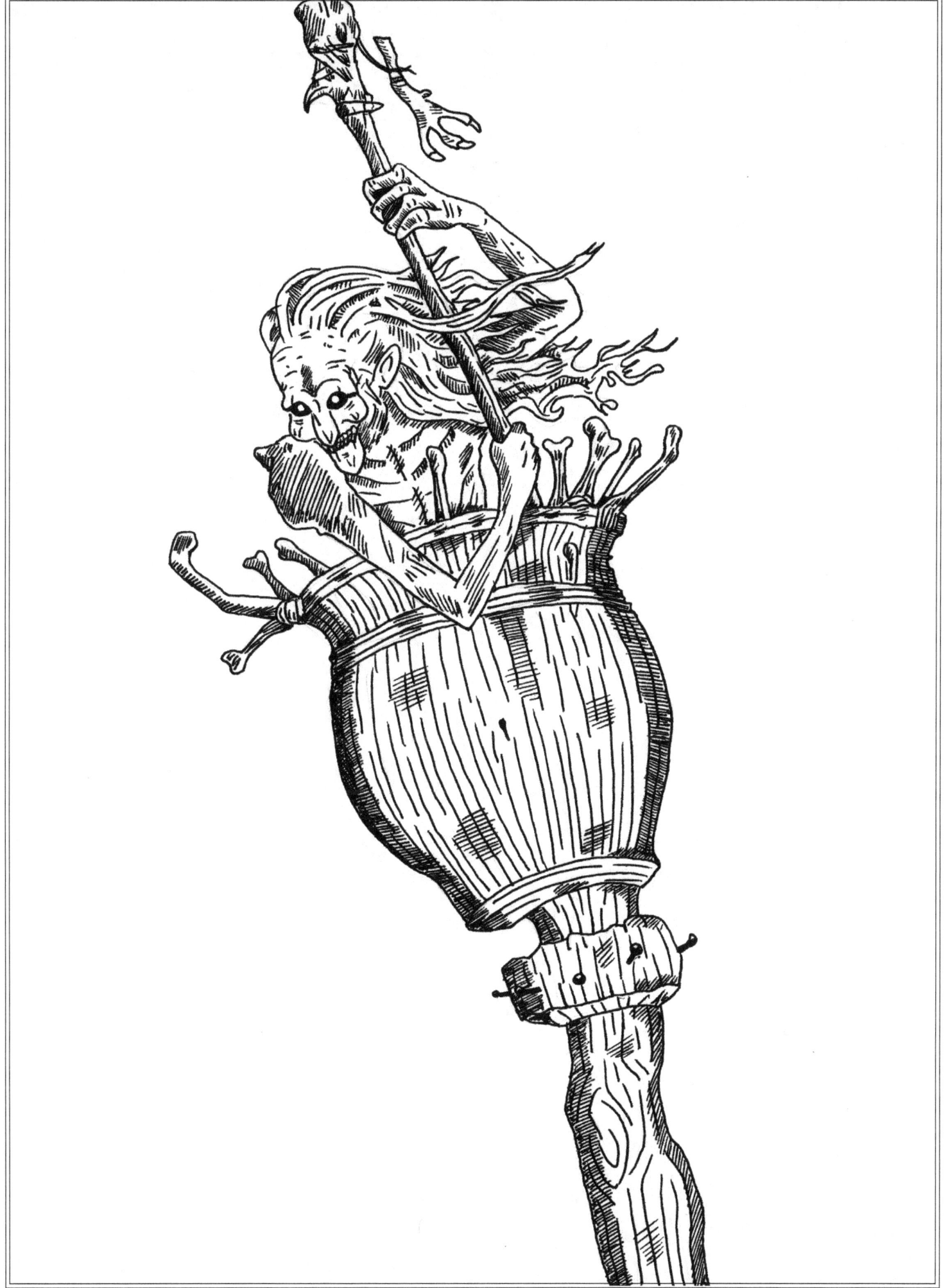

TISKYD Publishing

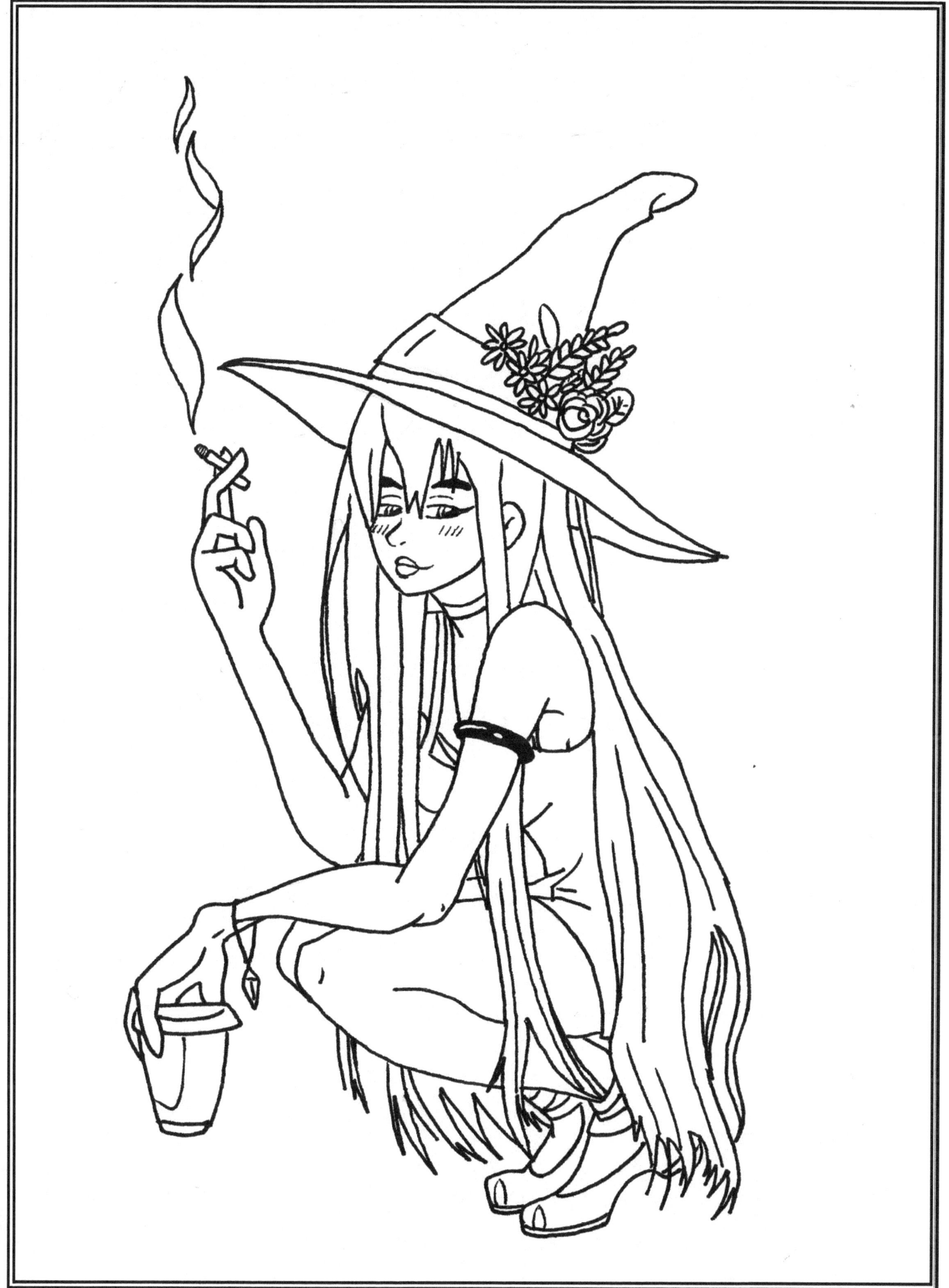

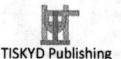

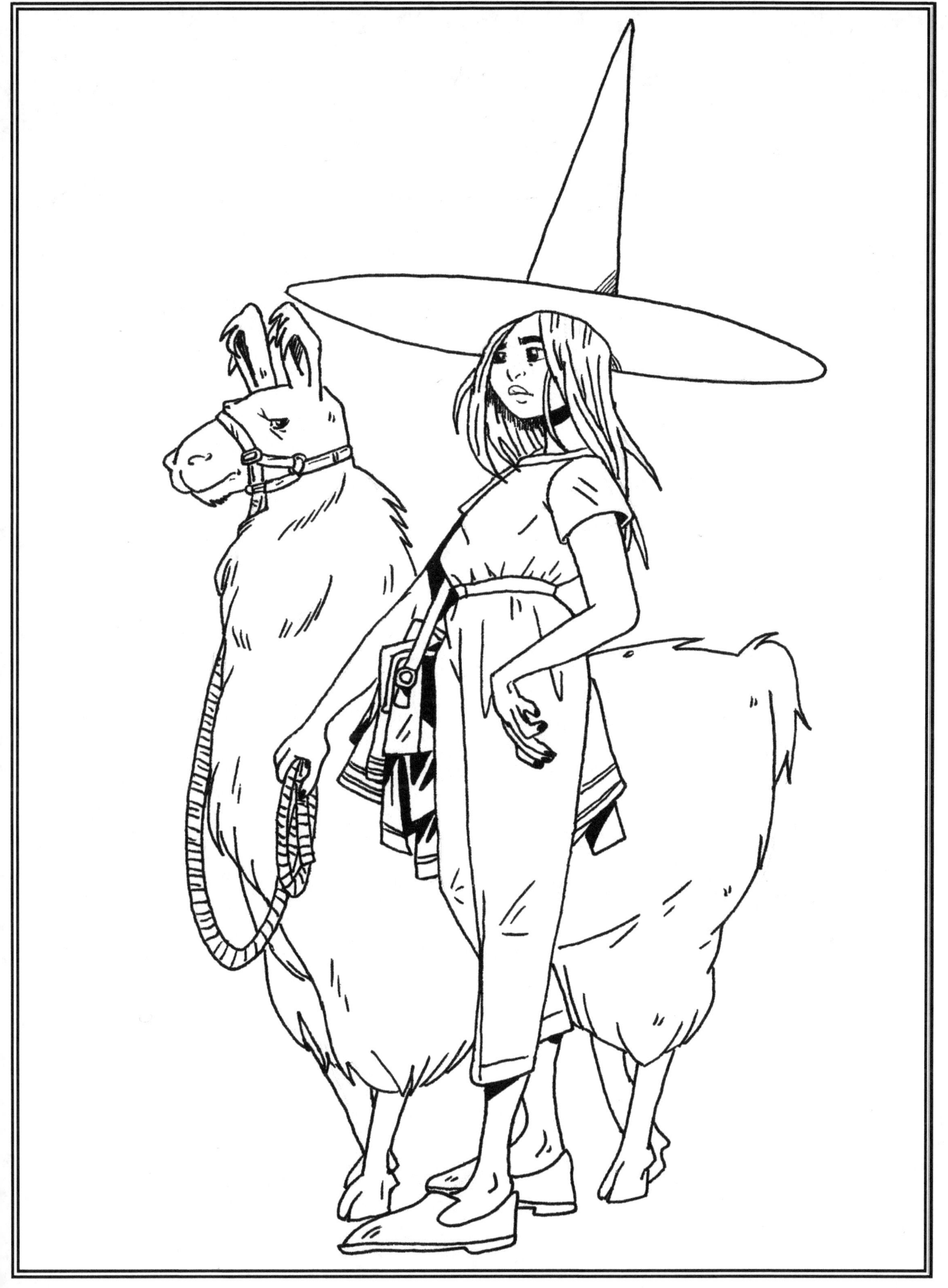

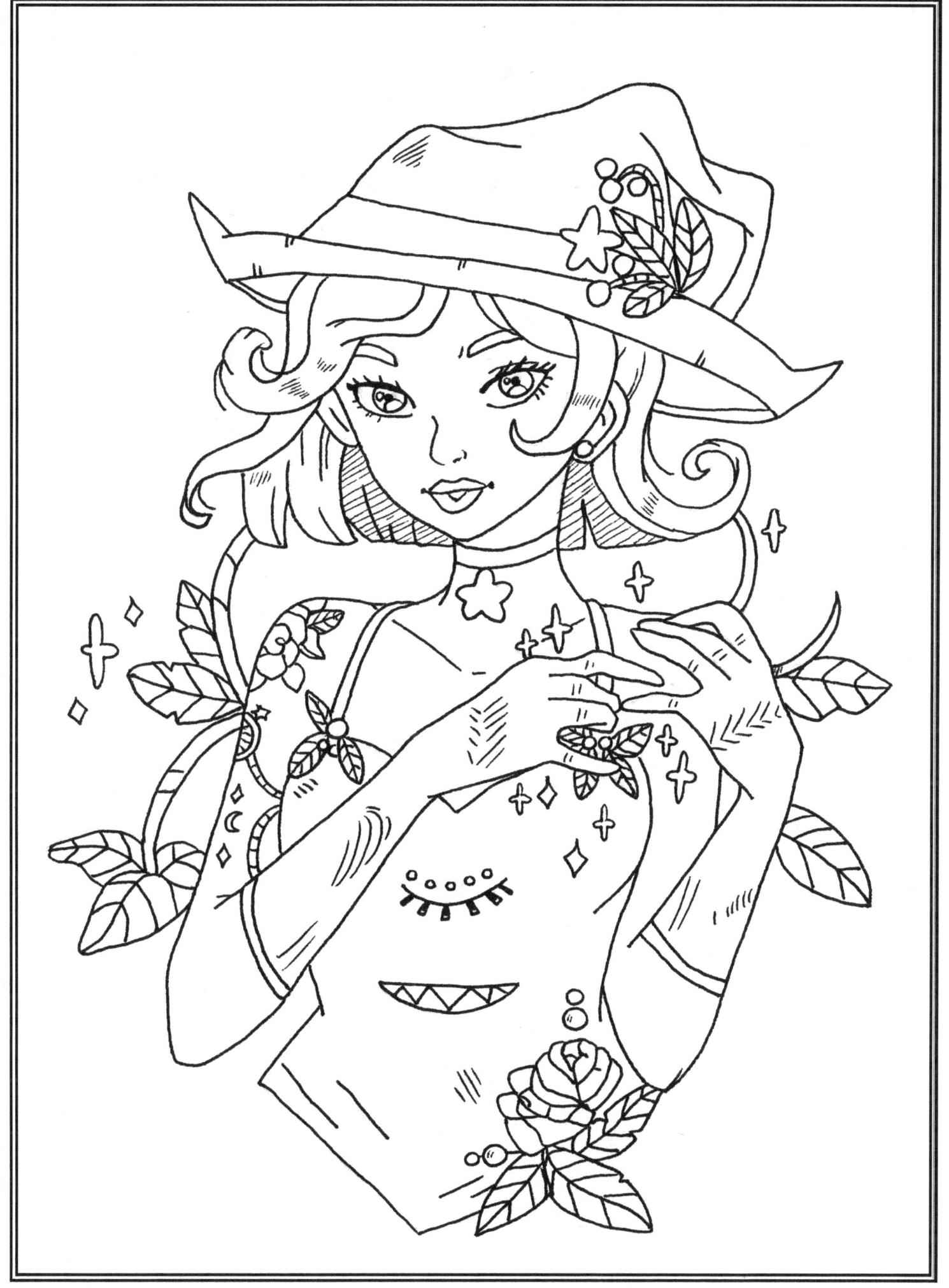

TISKYD Publishing

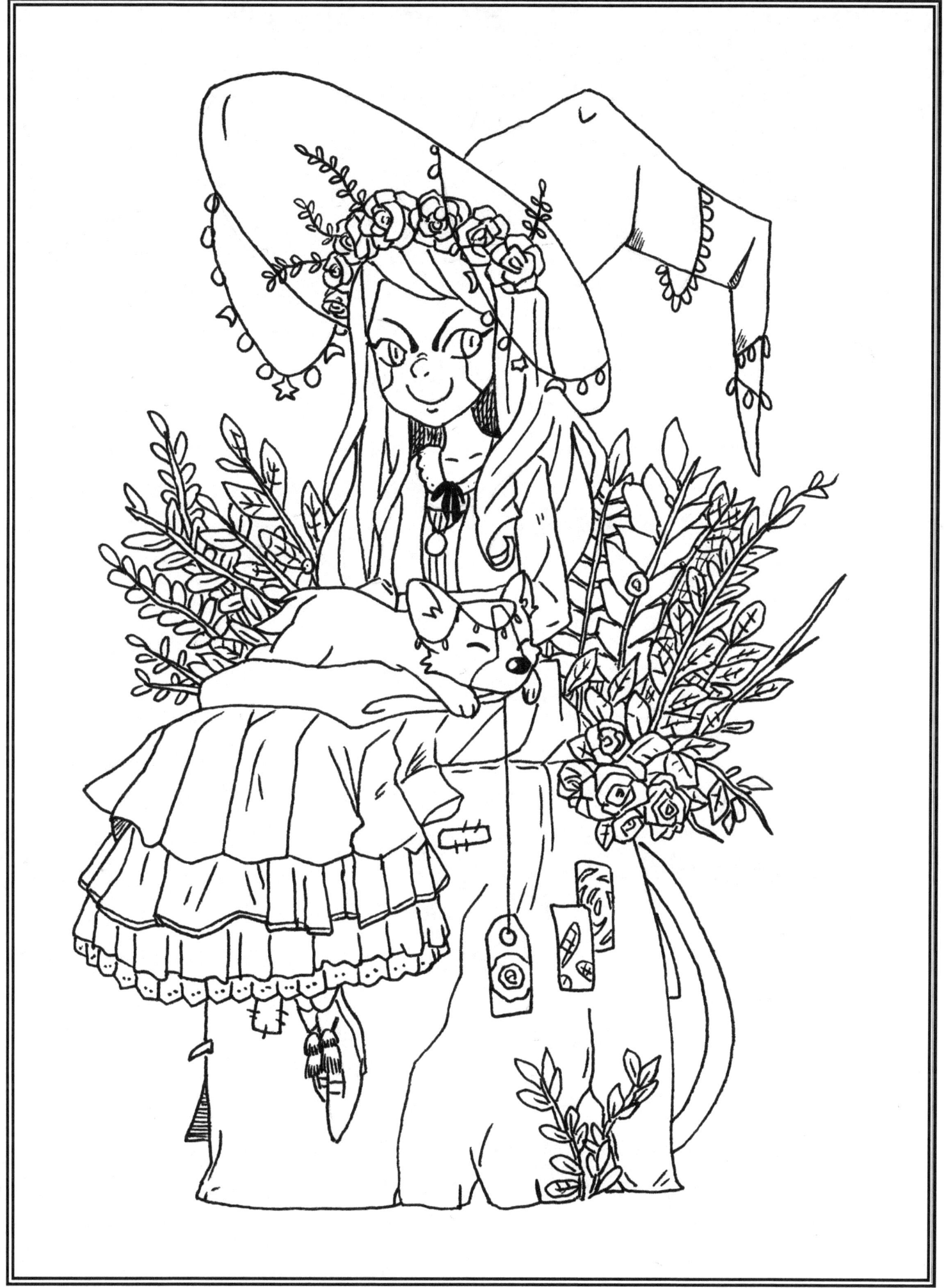

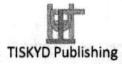
TISKYD Publishing

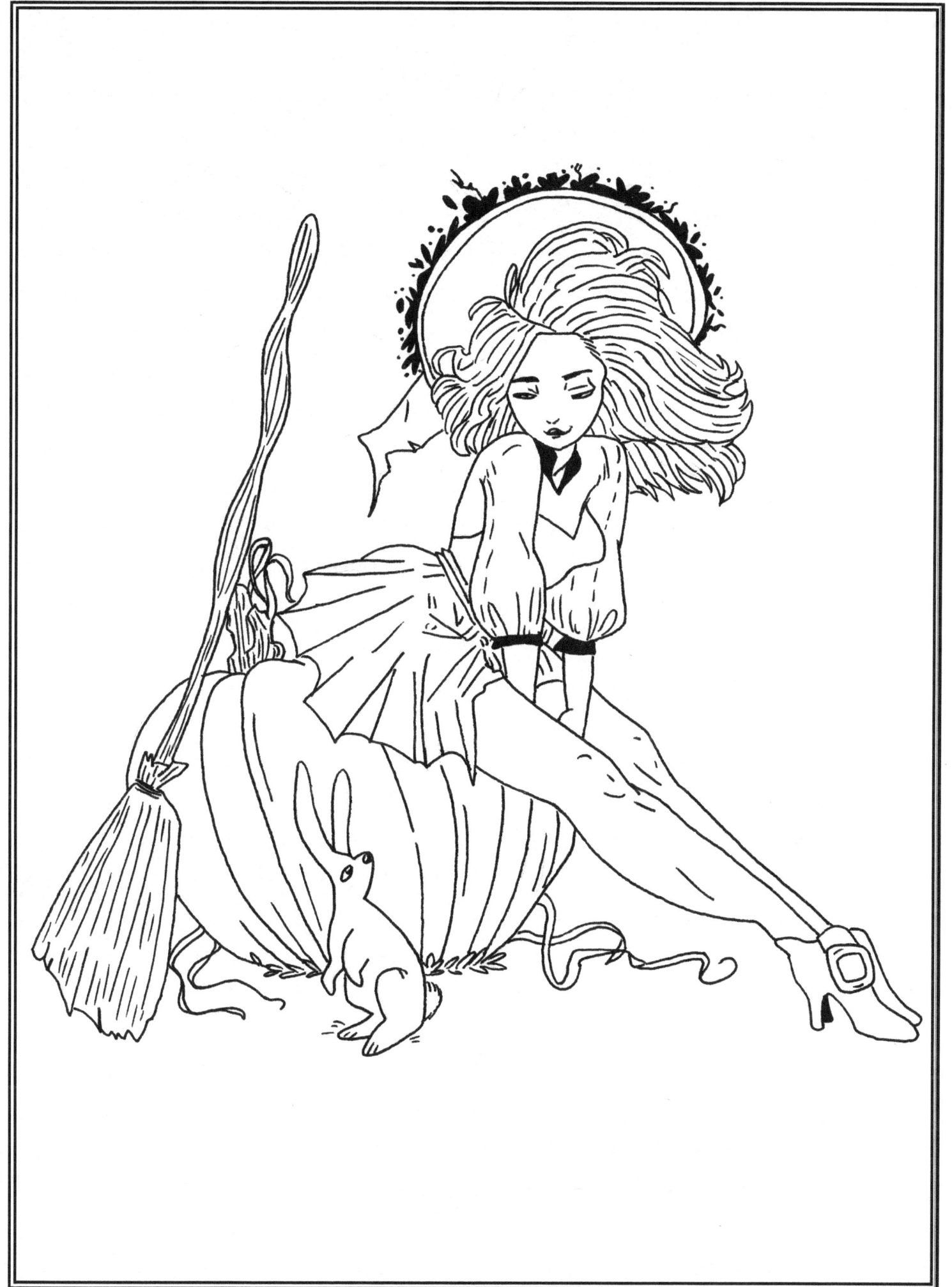

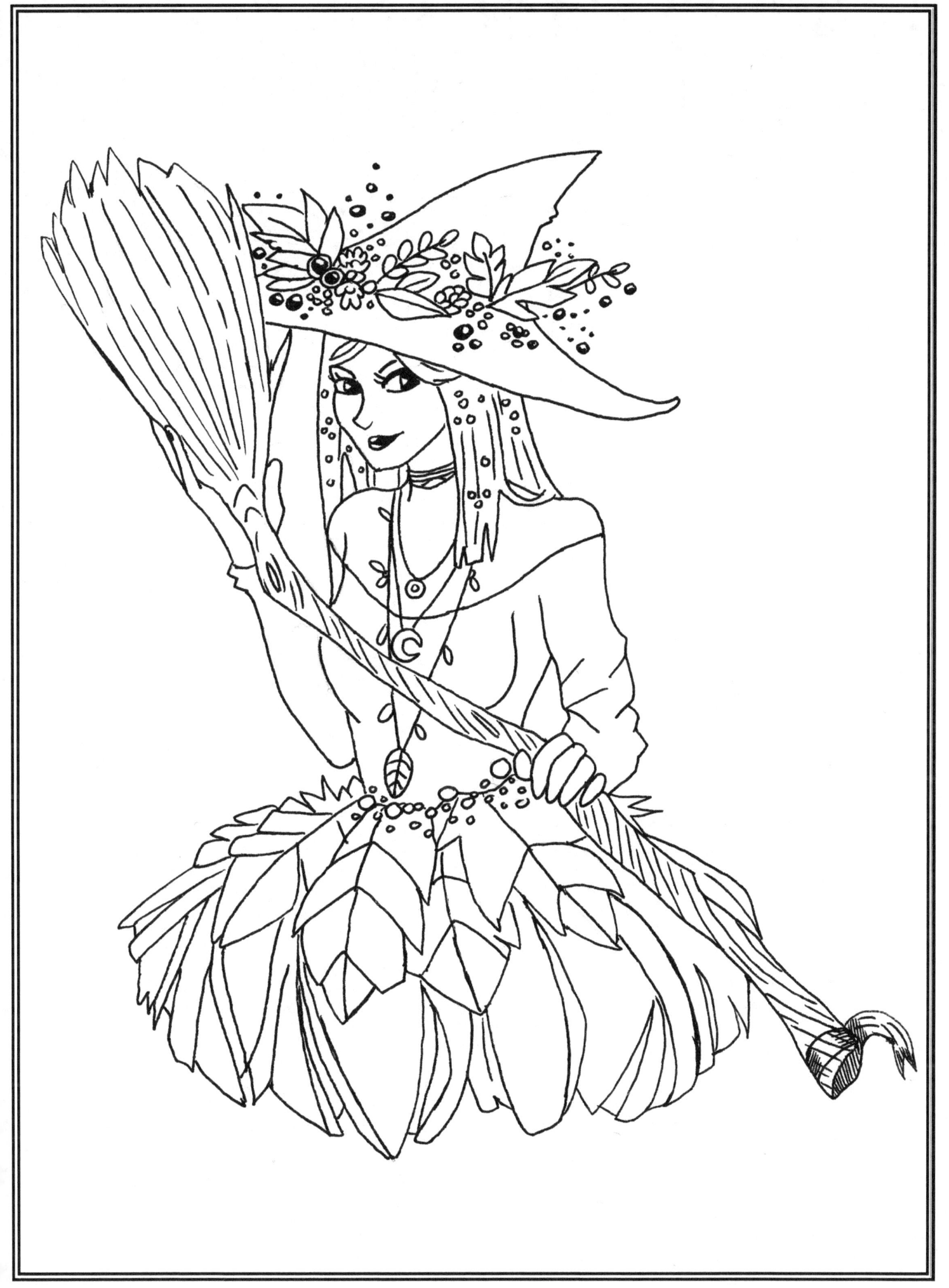

TISKYD Publishing

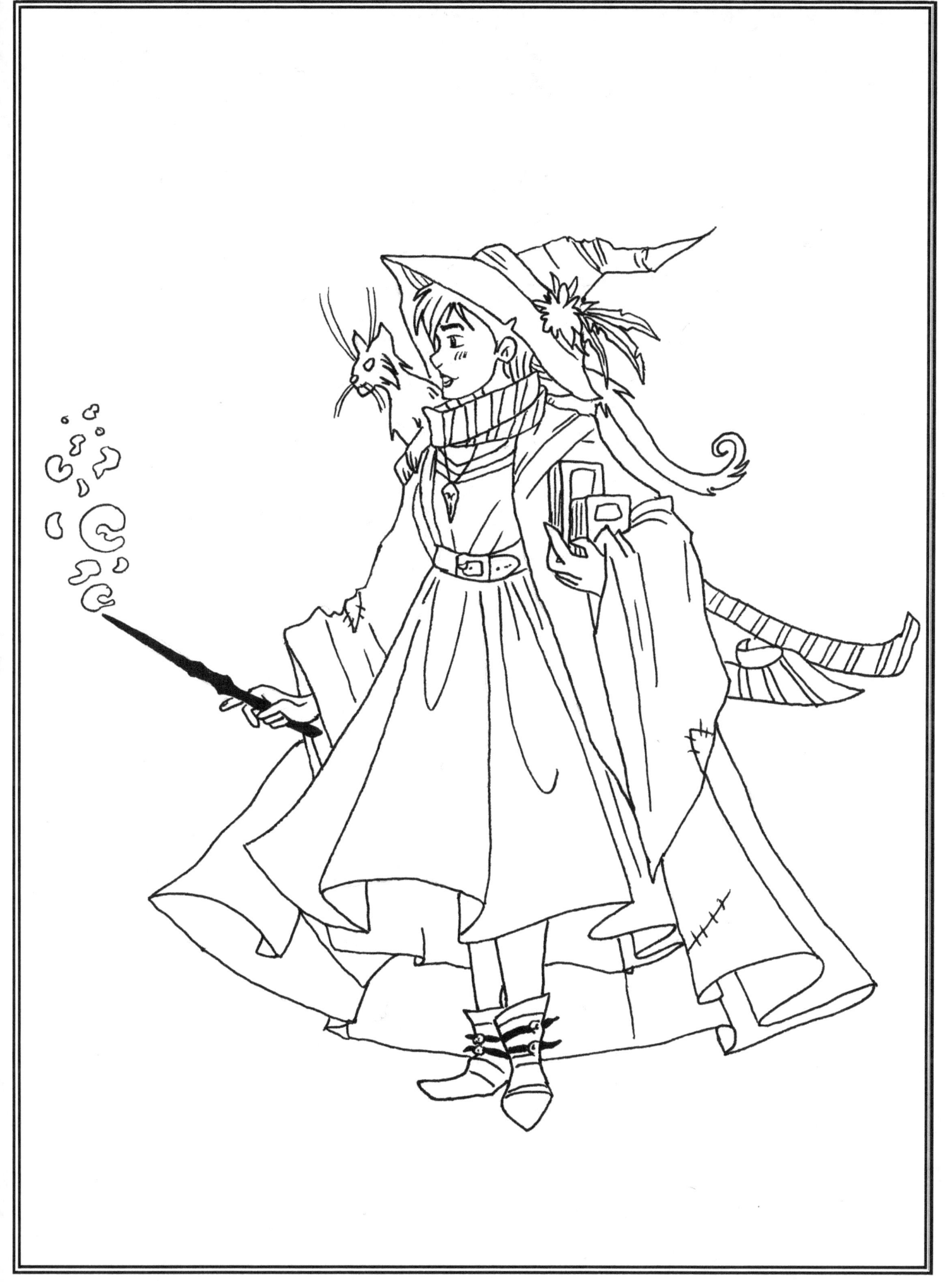

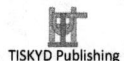

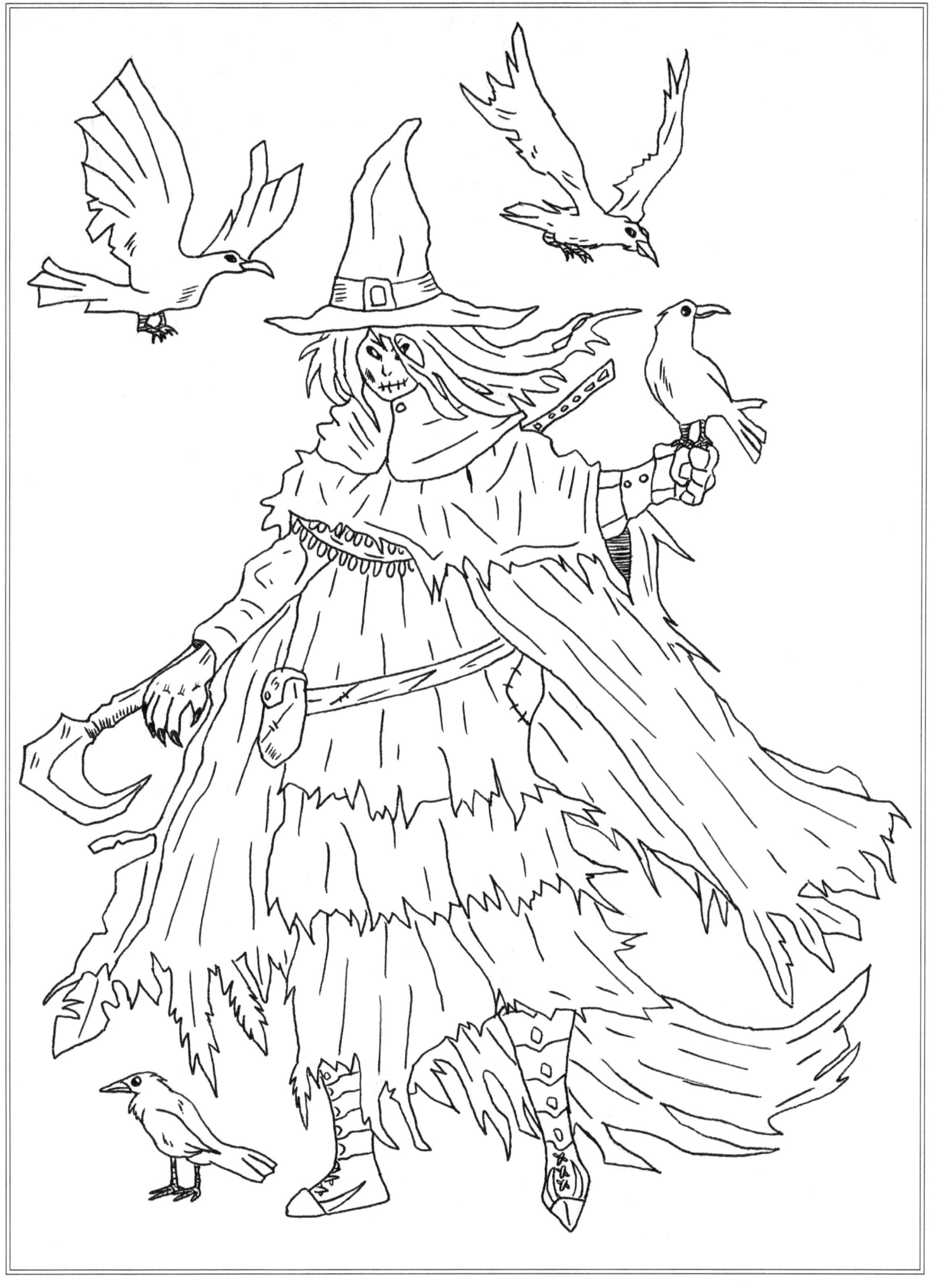

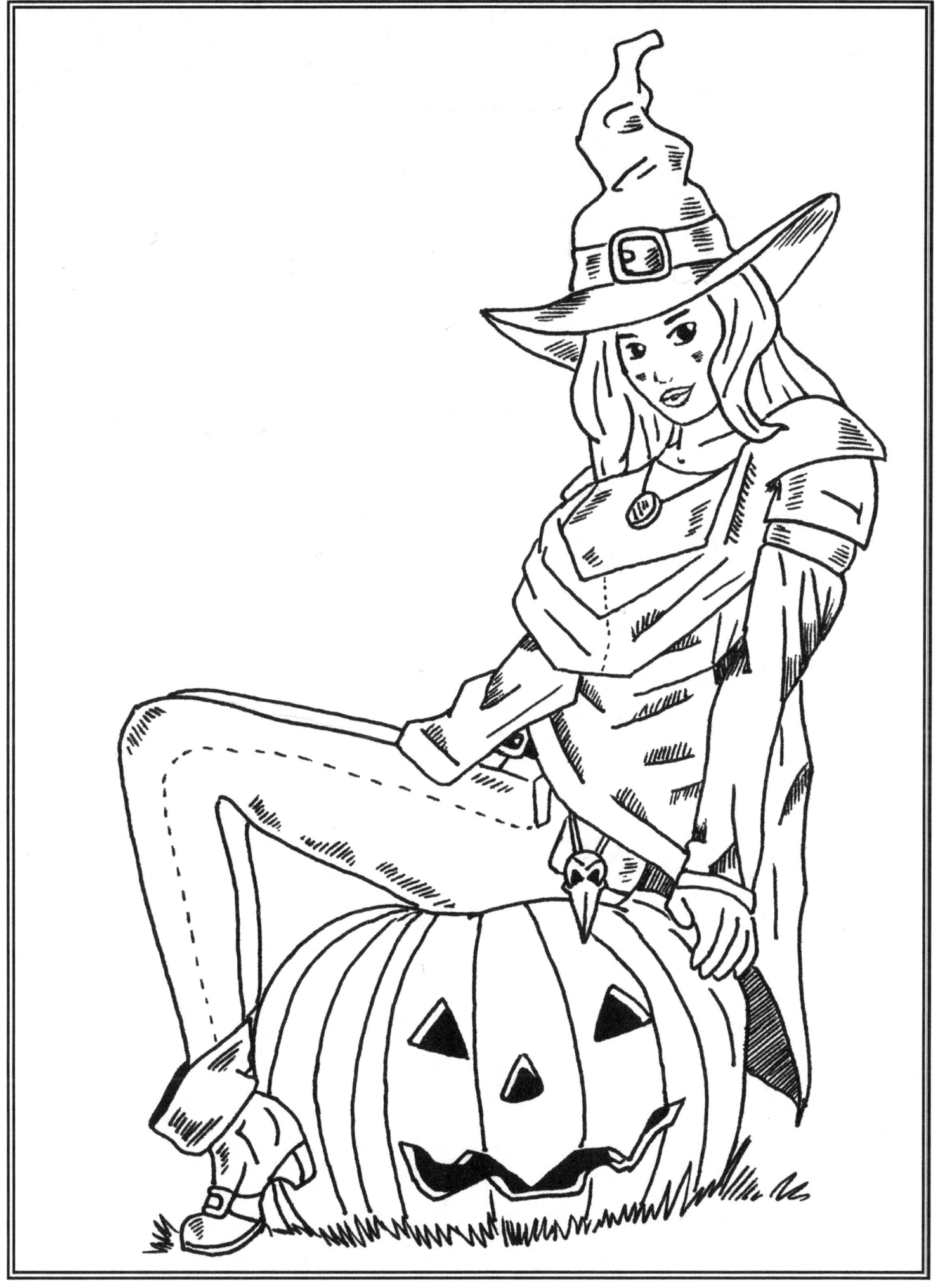

TISKYD Publishing

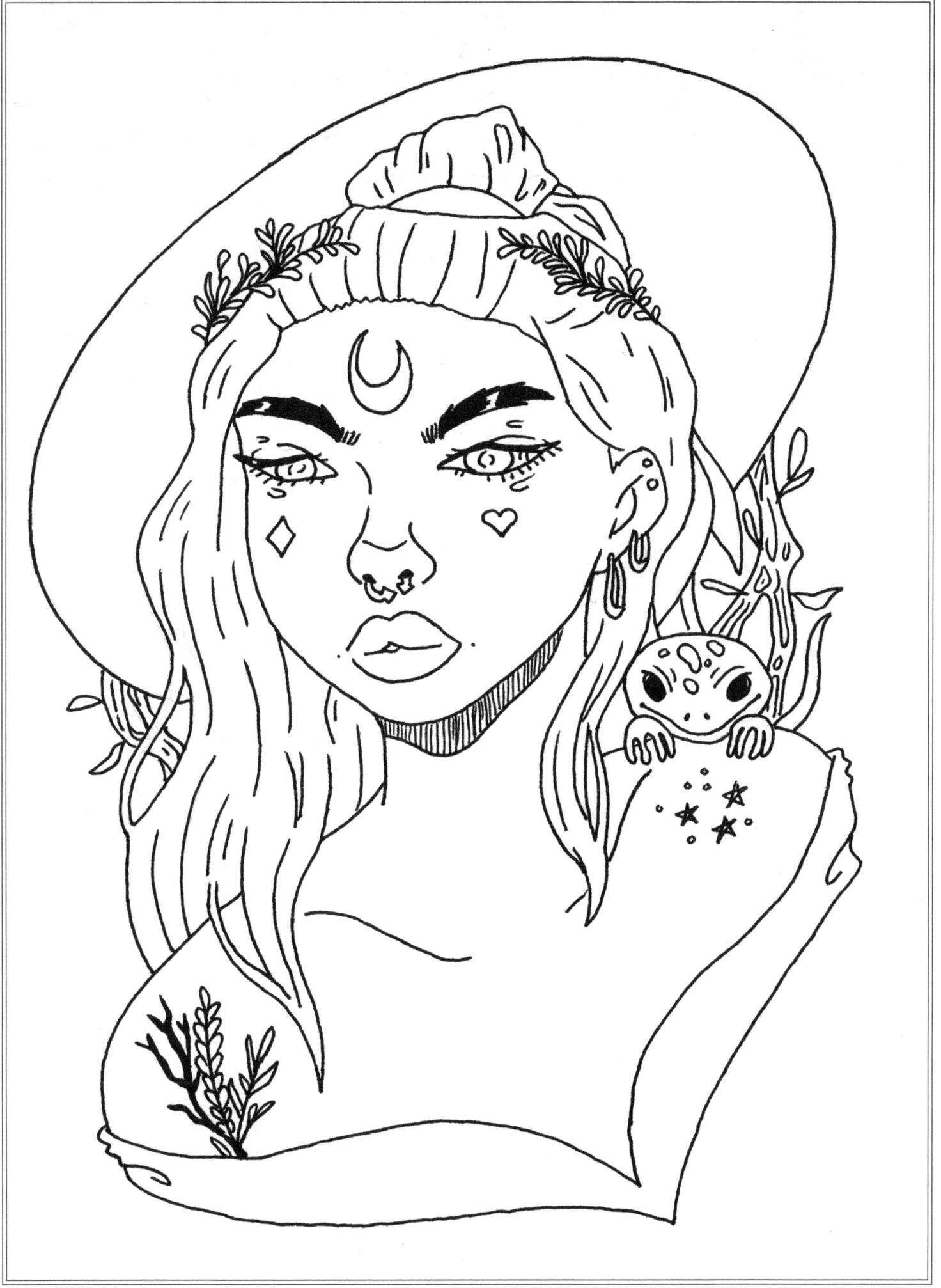

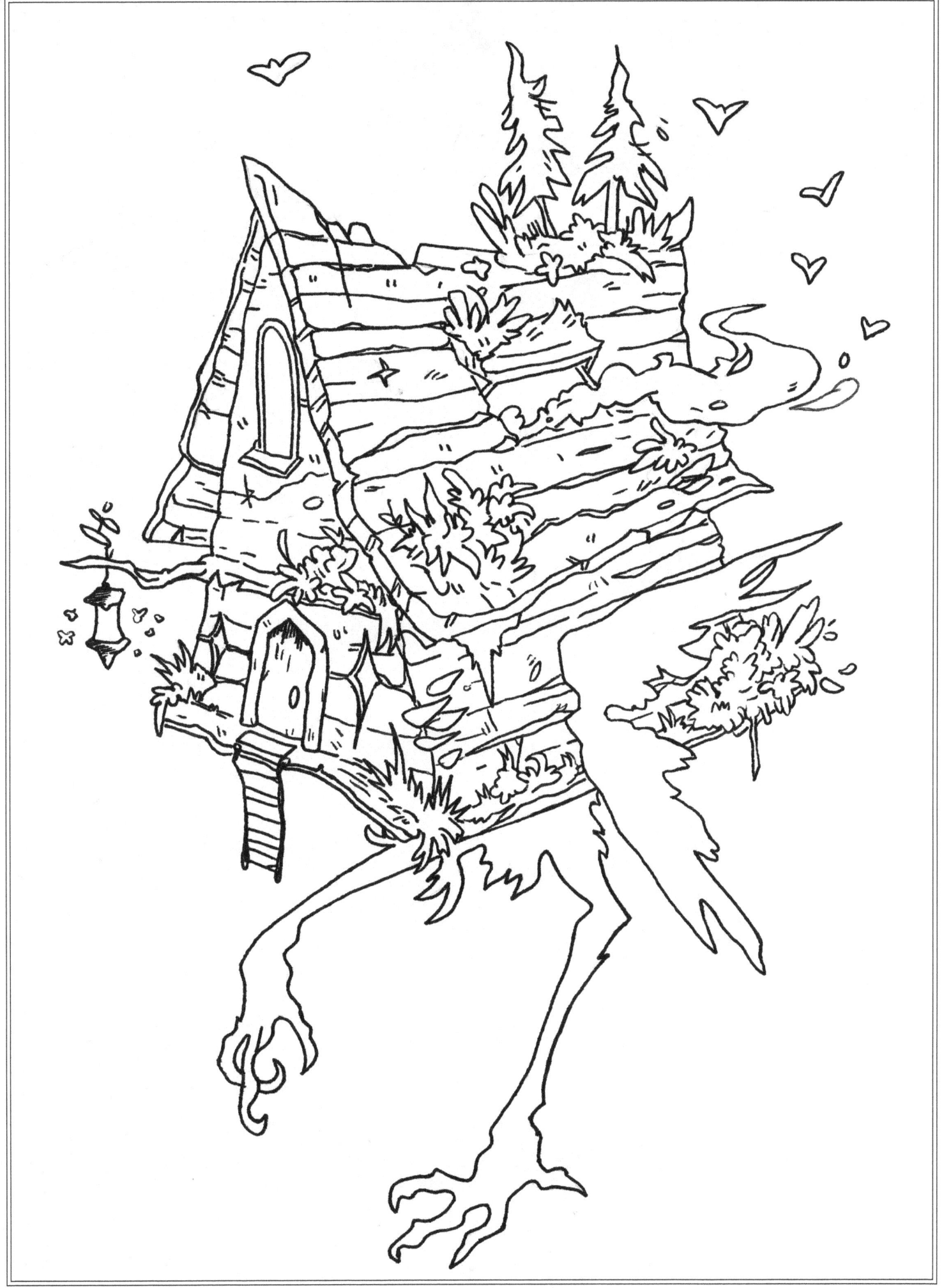

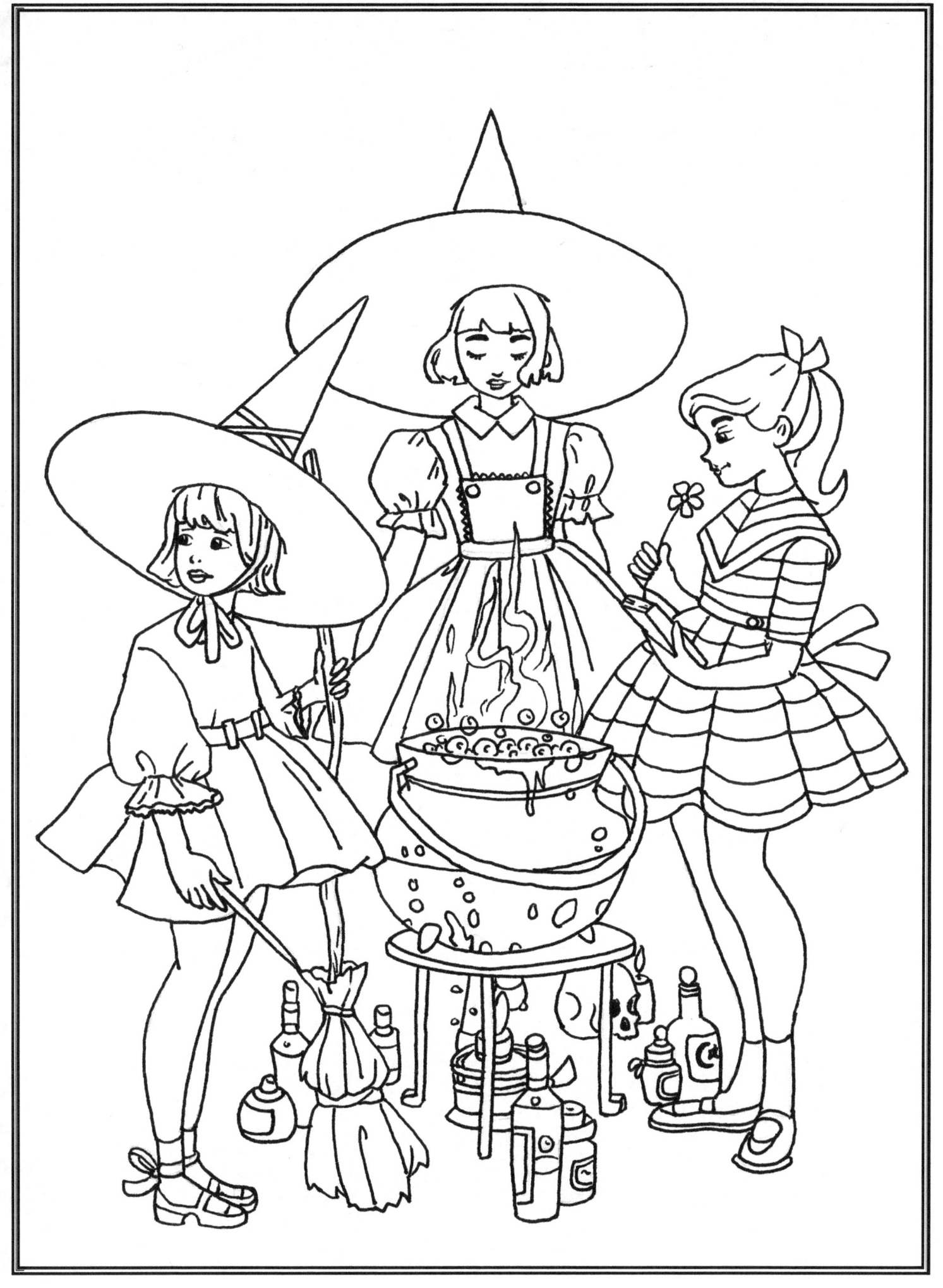

TISKYD Publishing

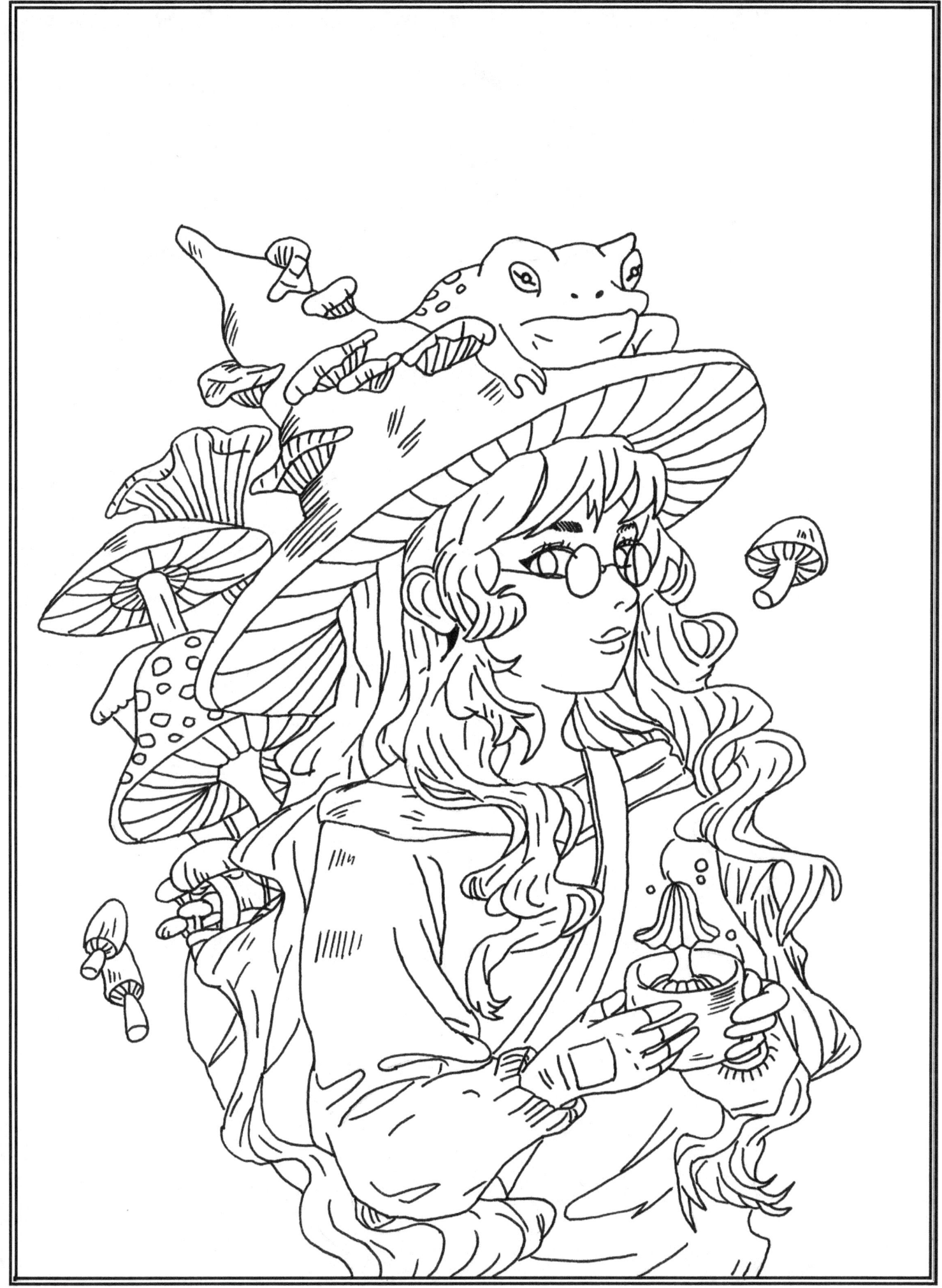

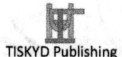

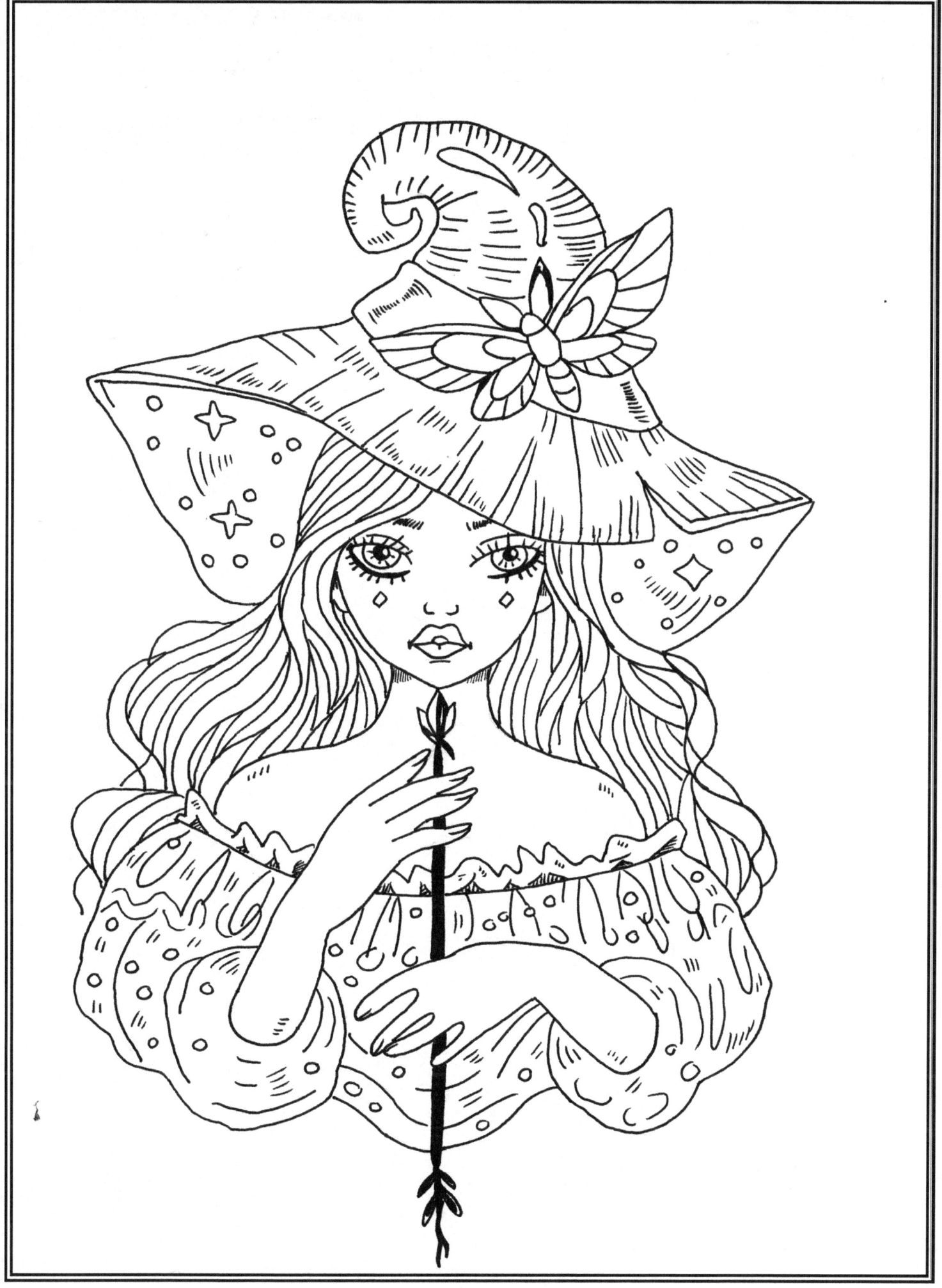

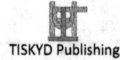
TISKYD Publishing

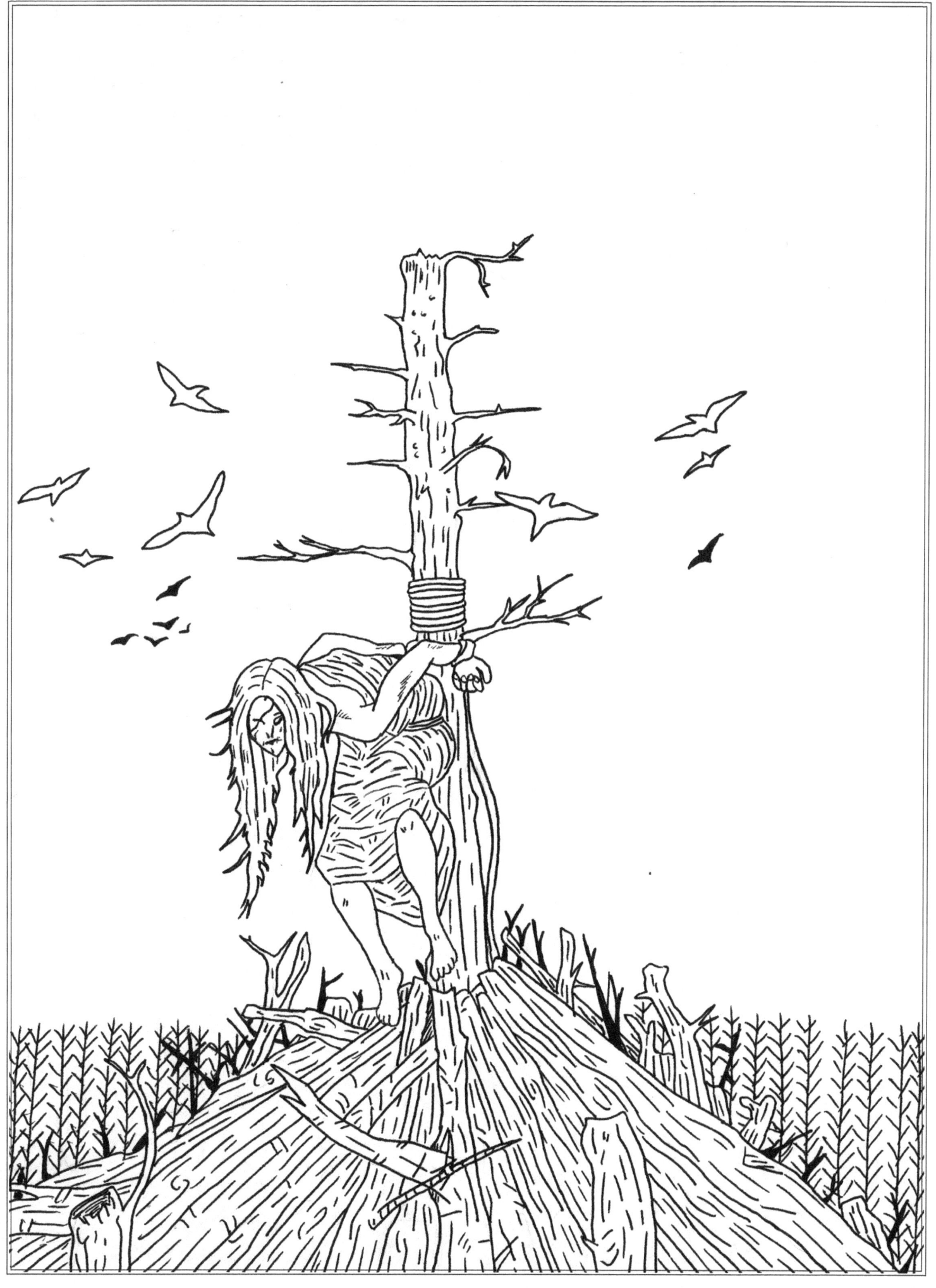

TISKYD Publishing

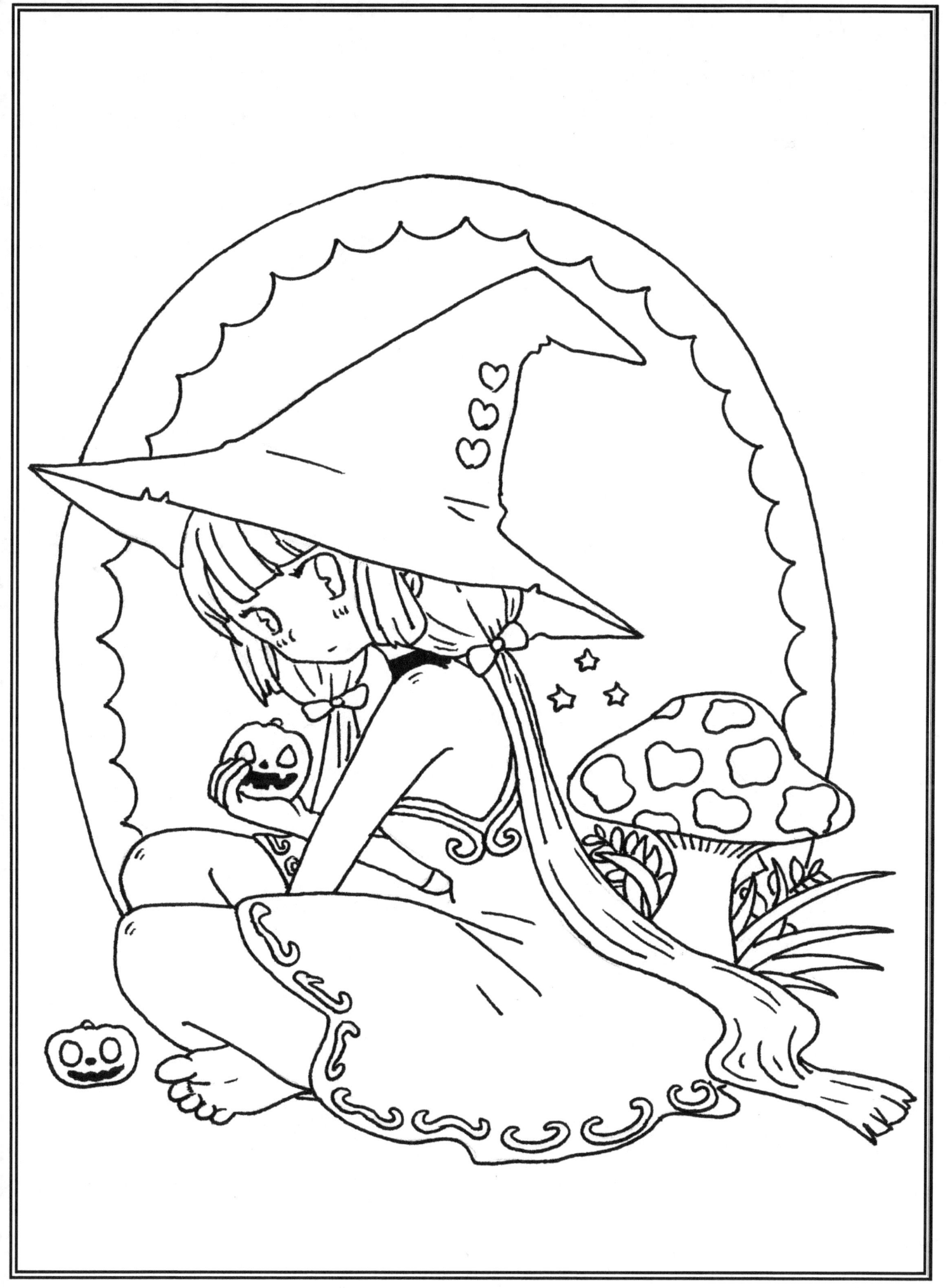

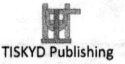

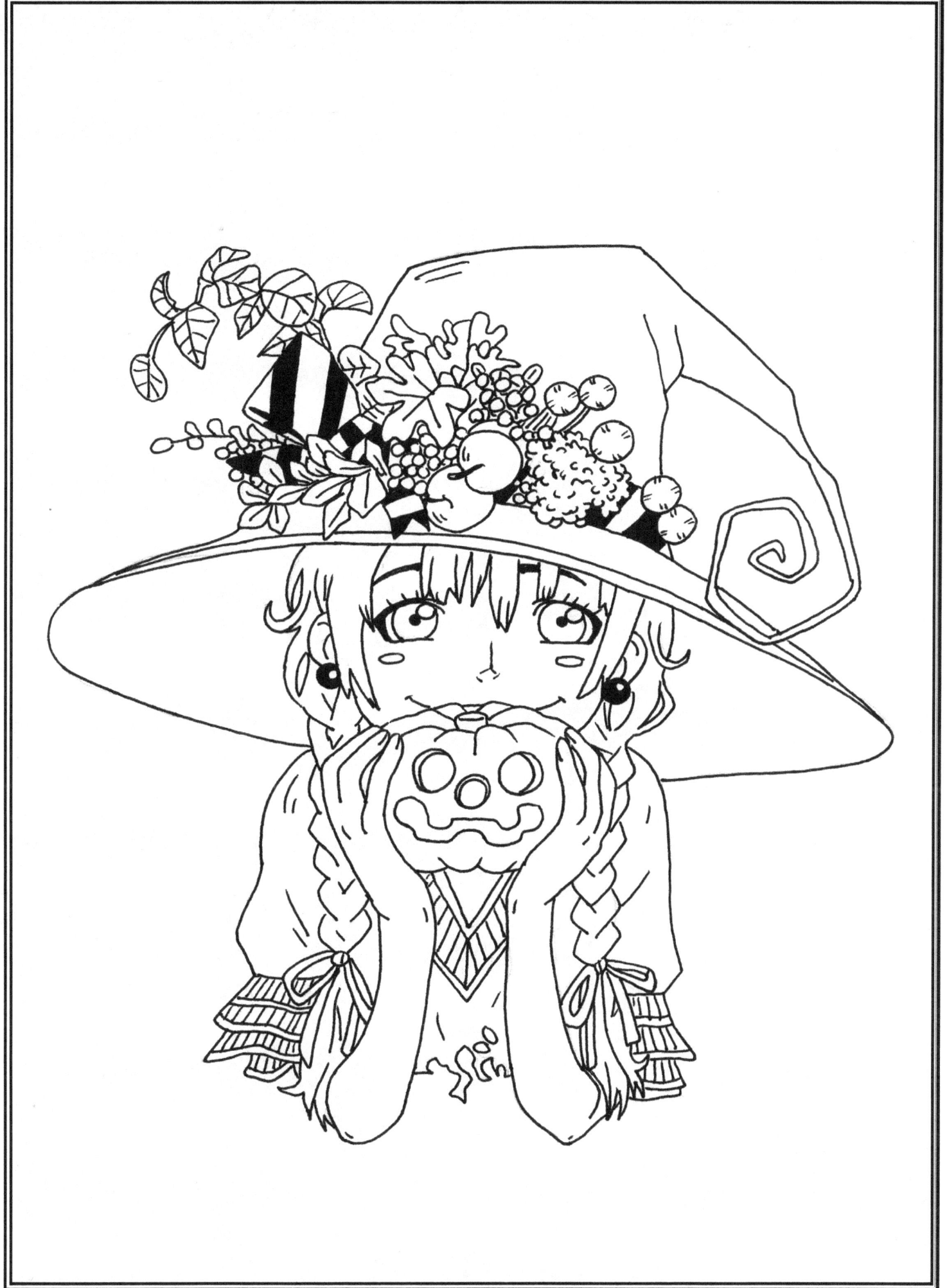

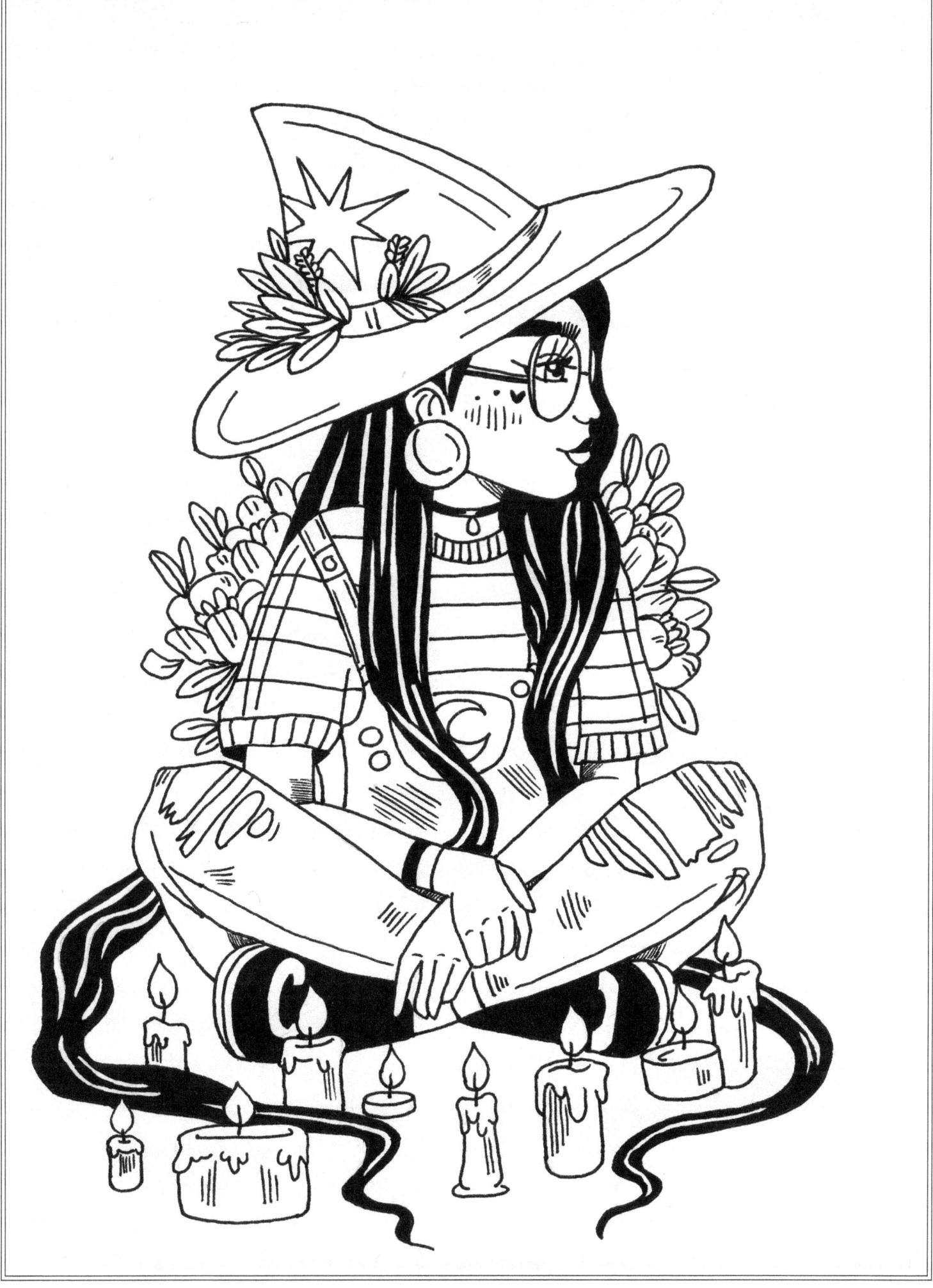

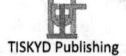

TISKYD Publishing

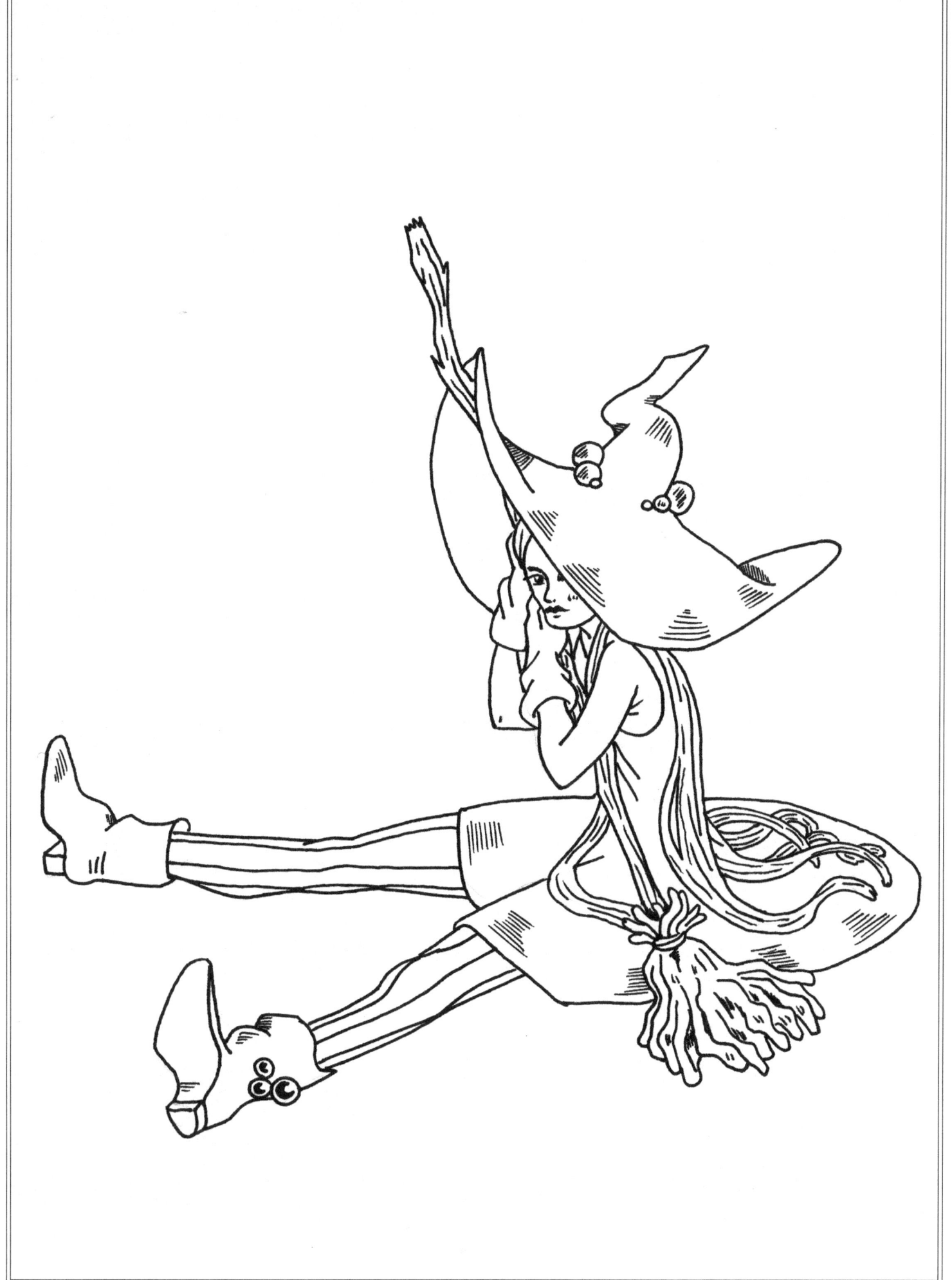

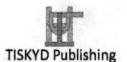

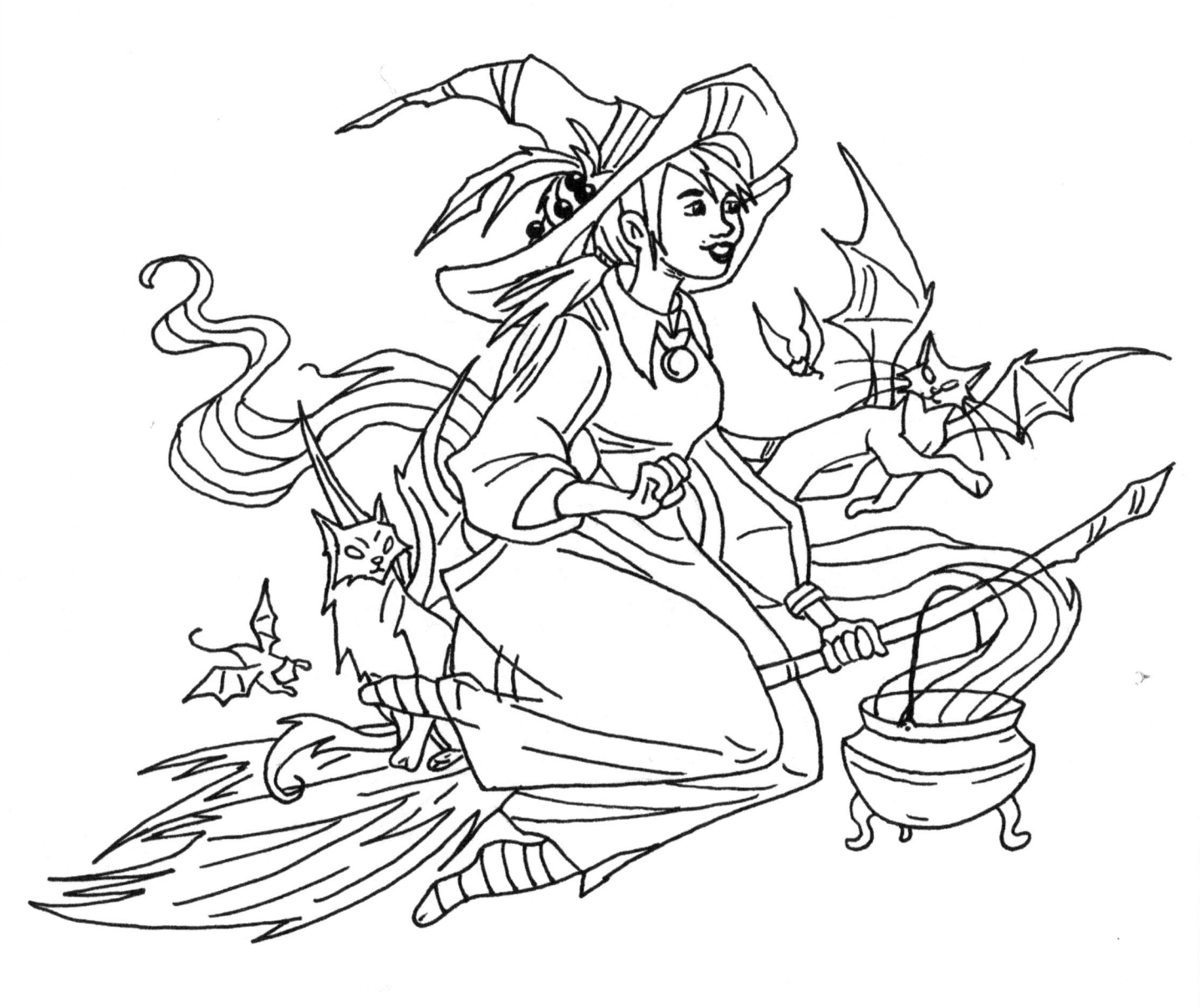

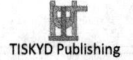
TISKYD Publishing

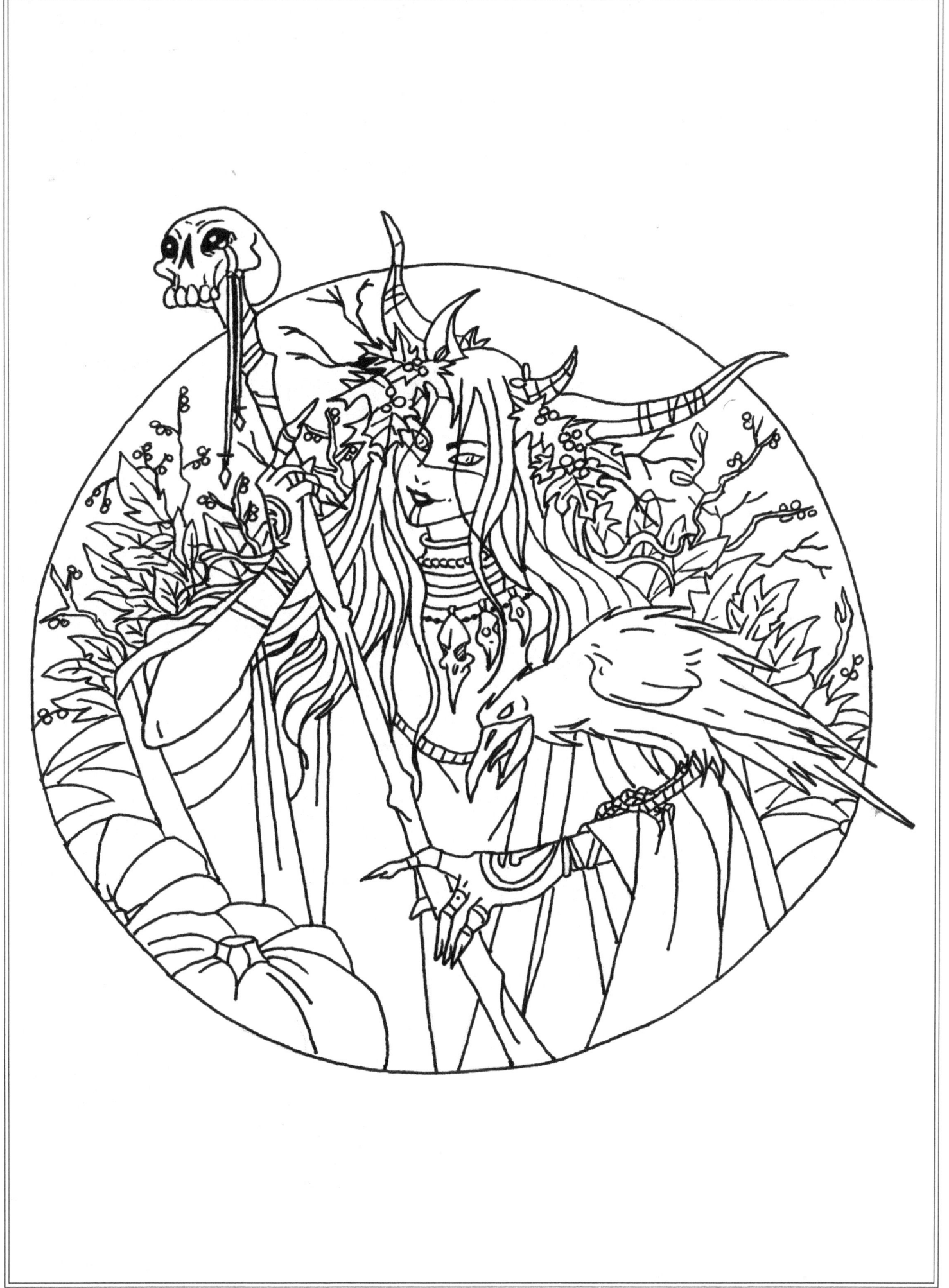

TISKYD Publishing

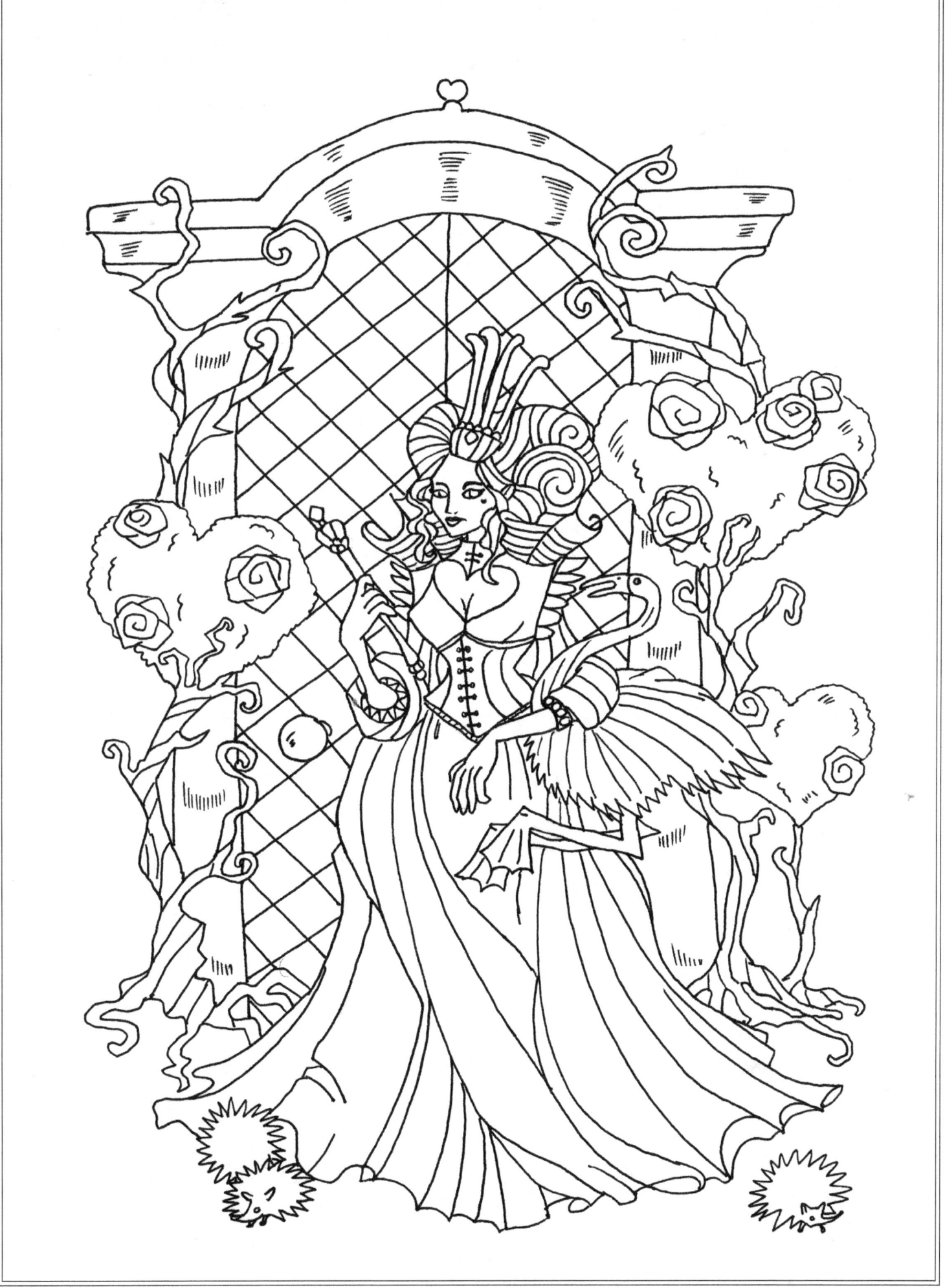

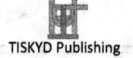
TISKYD Publishing

The subsequent section comprises the previous images in a smaller version to let kids test colors and techniques before carrying on with the larger images.

TISKYD Publishing

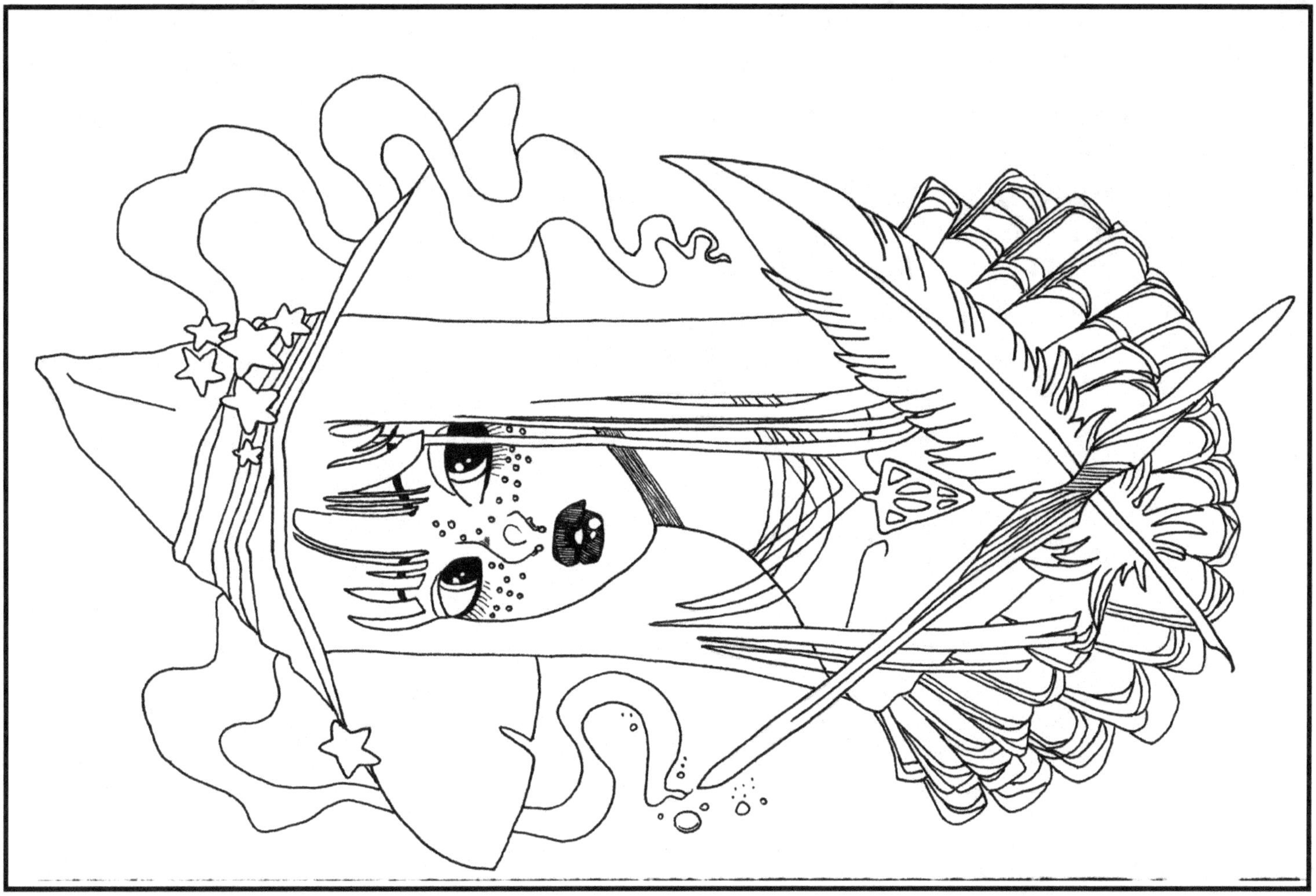

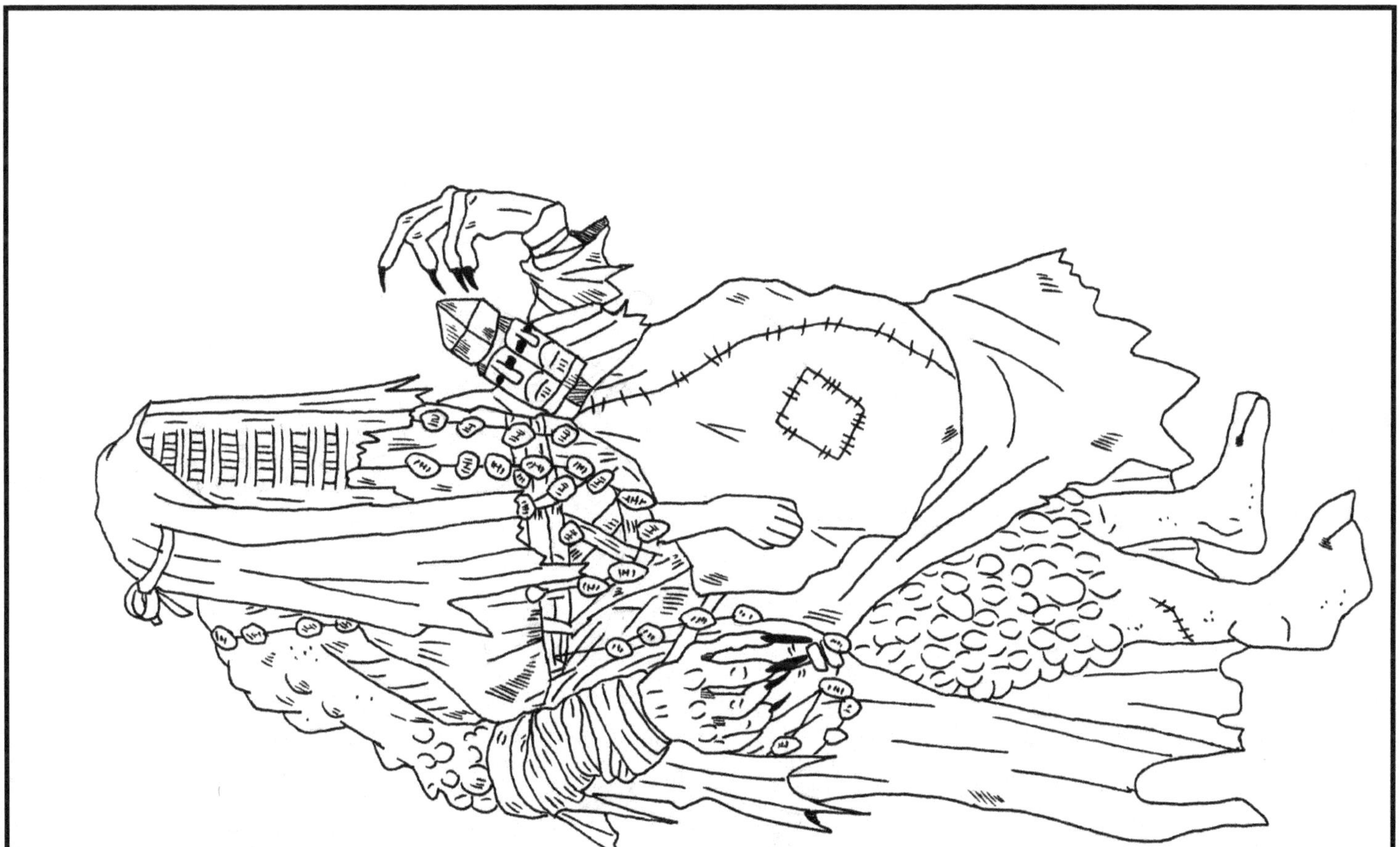

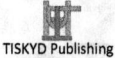

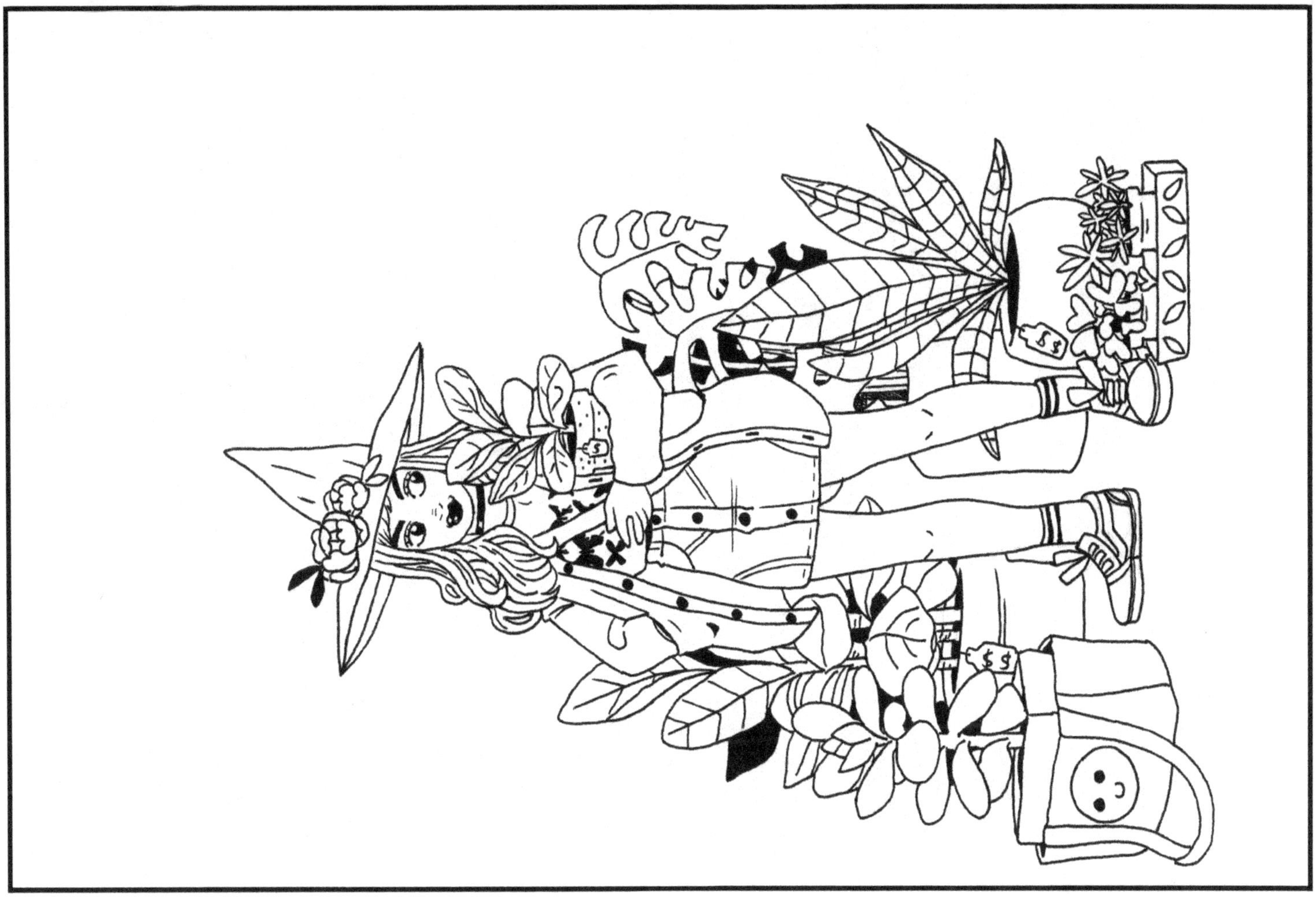

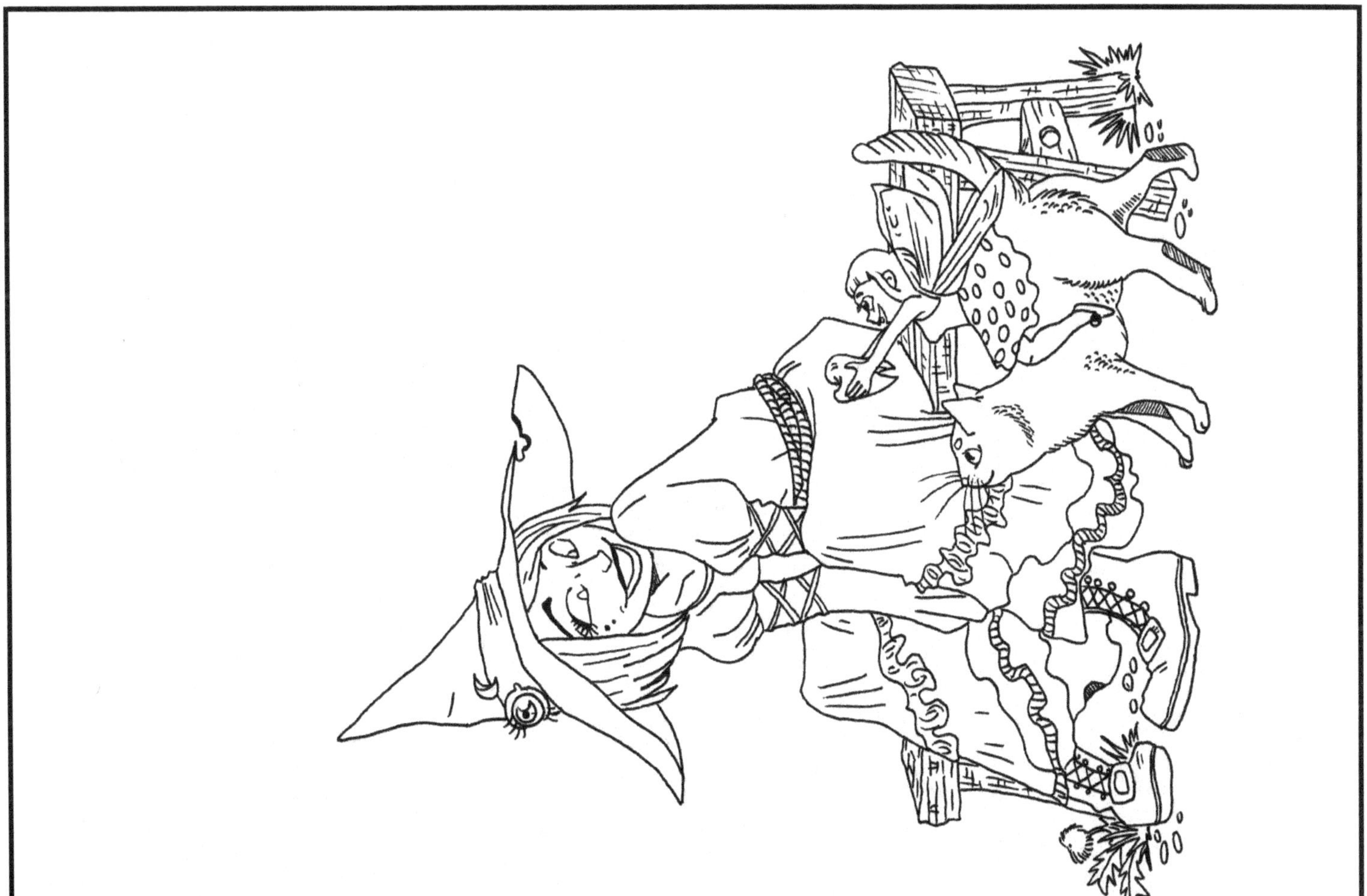

TISKYD Publishing

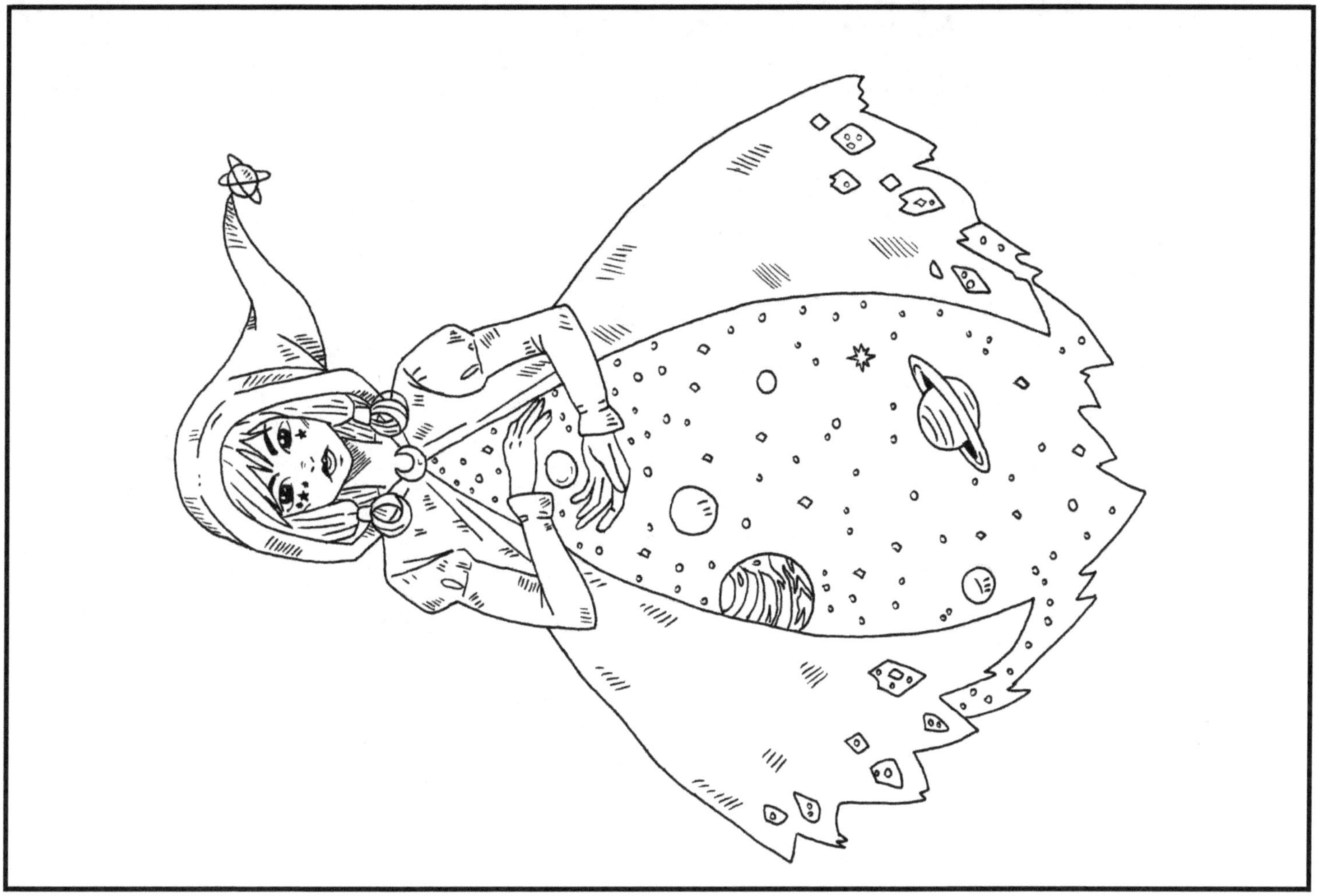

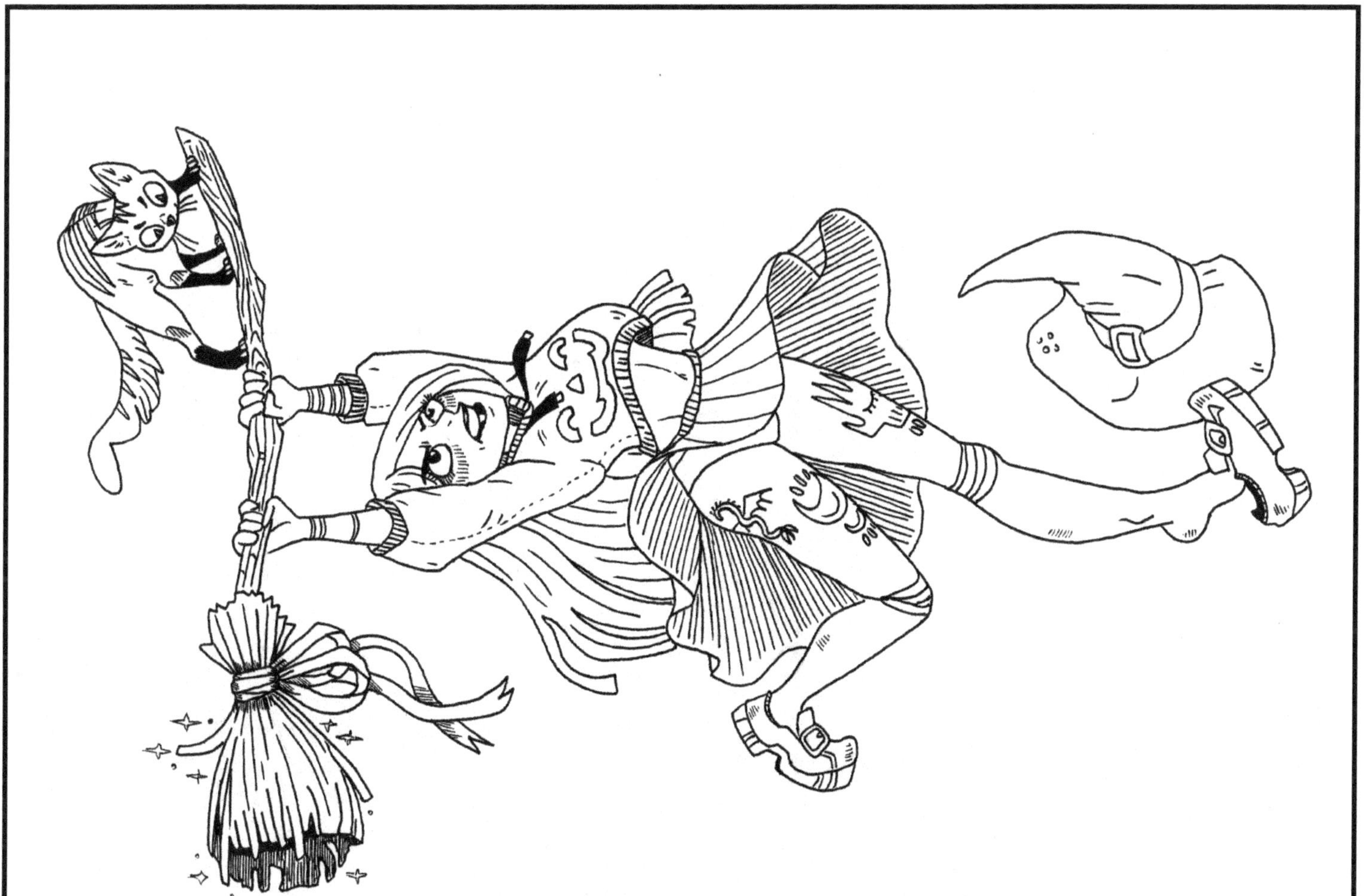

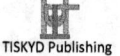
TISKYD Publishing

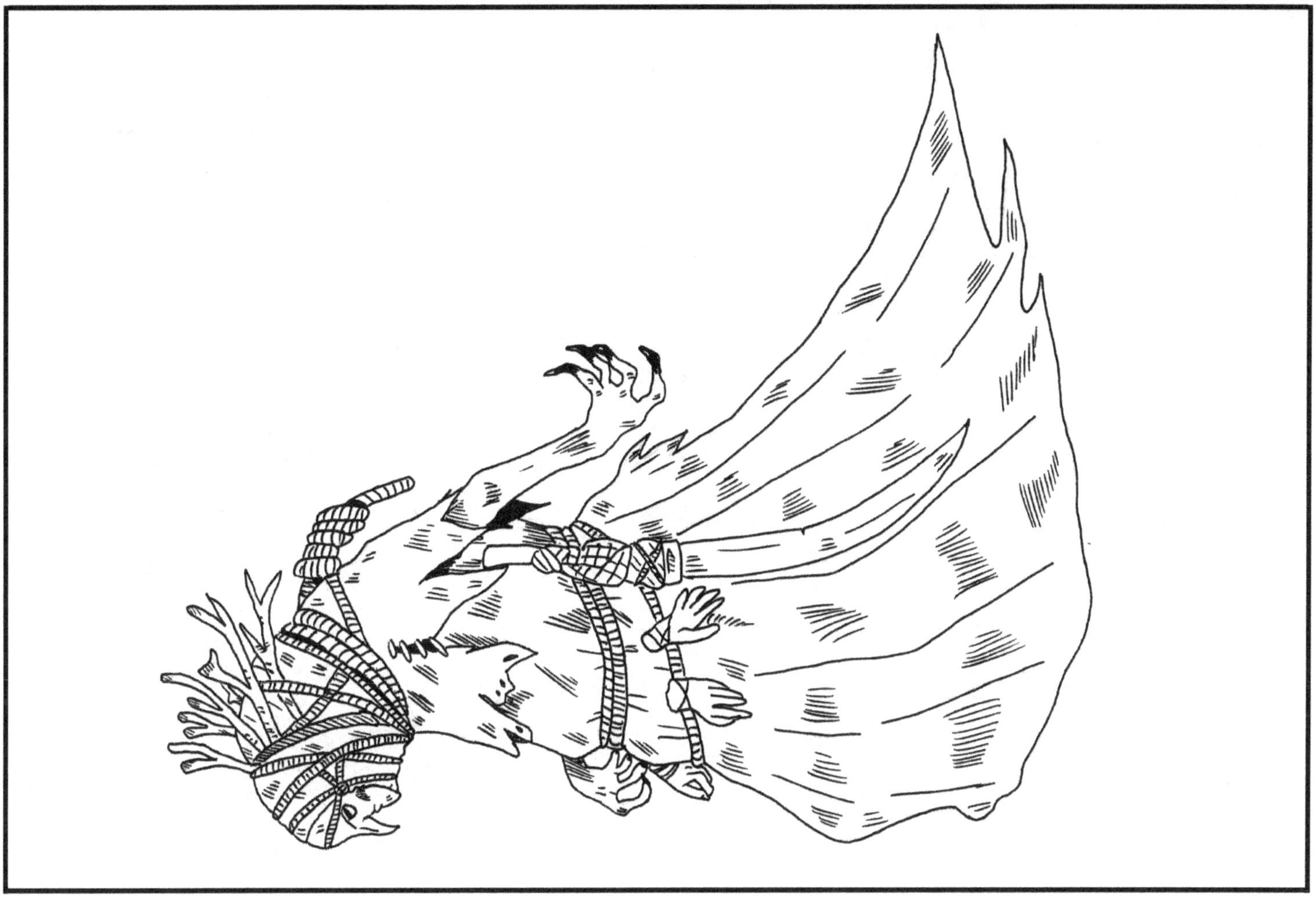

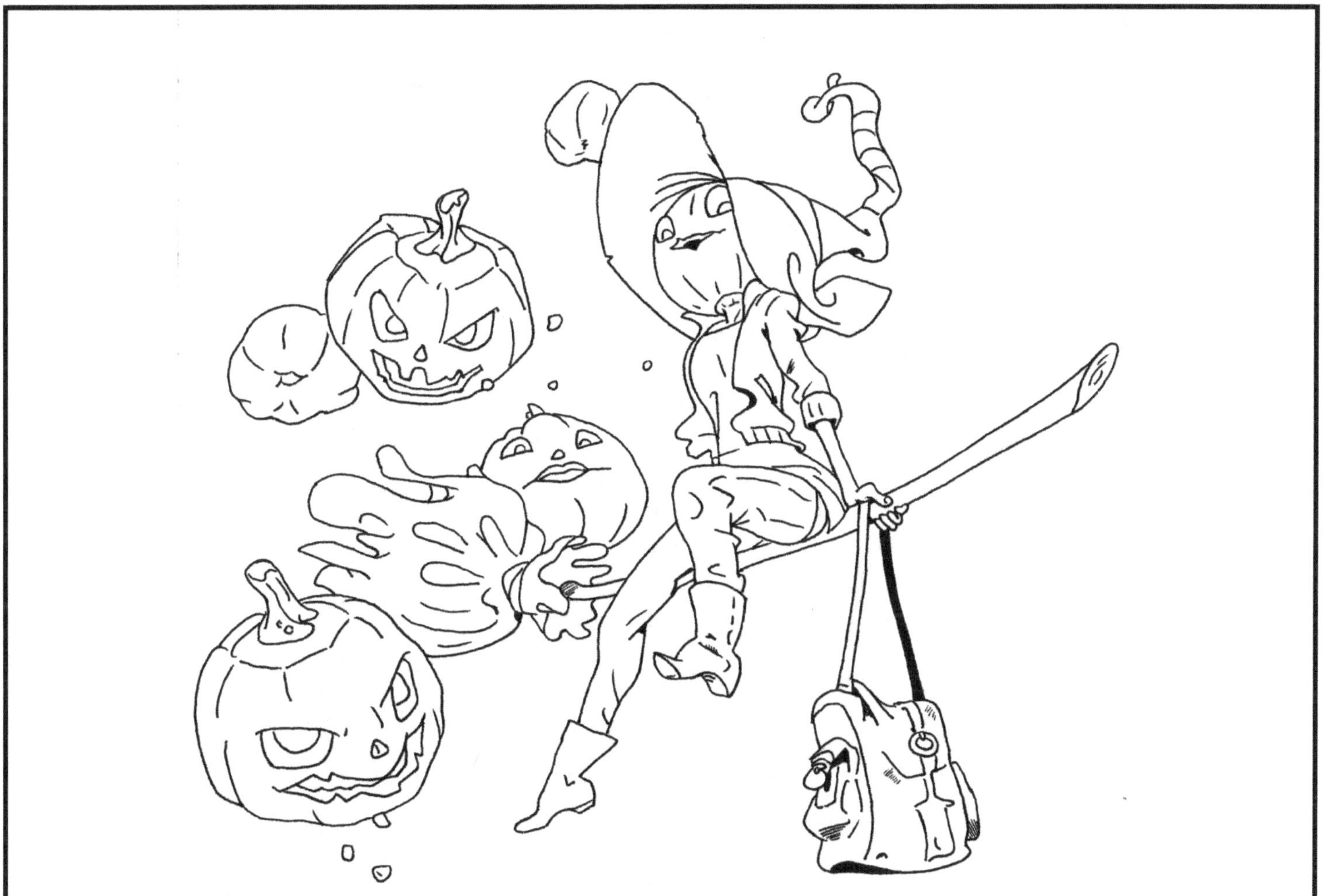

TISKYD Publishing

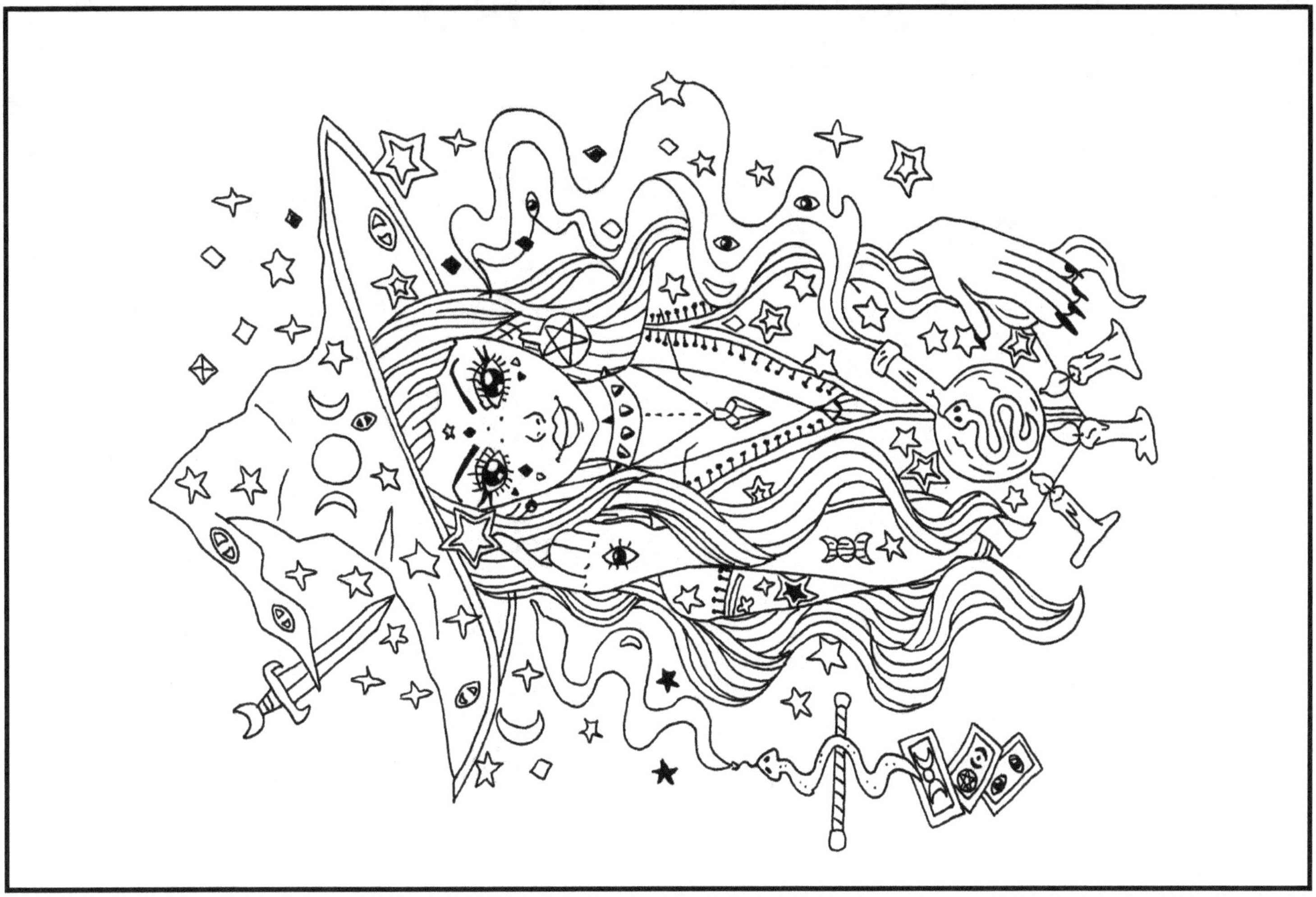

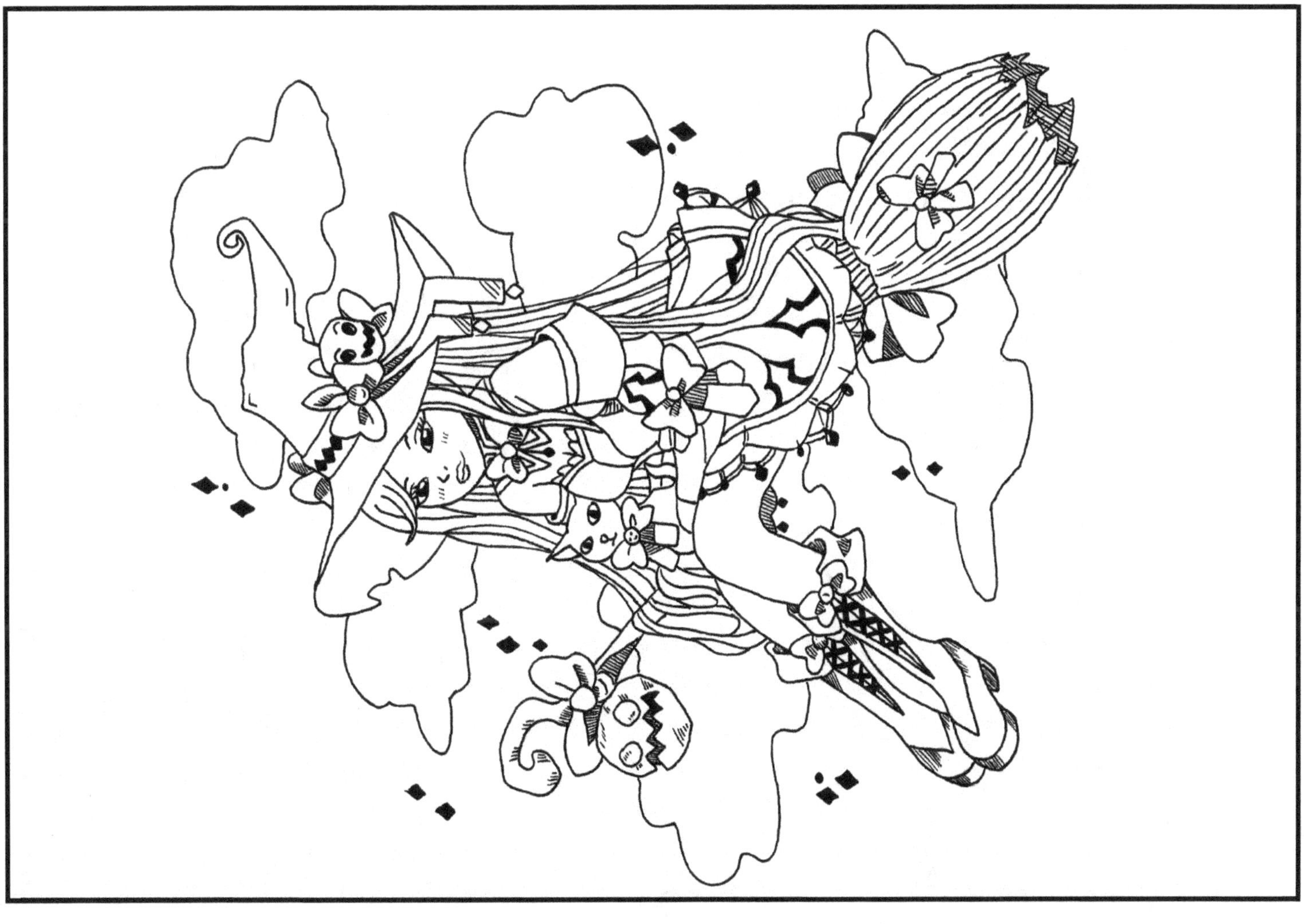

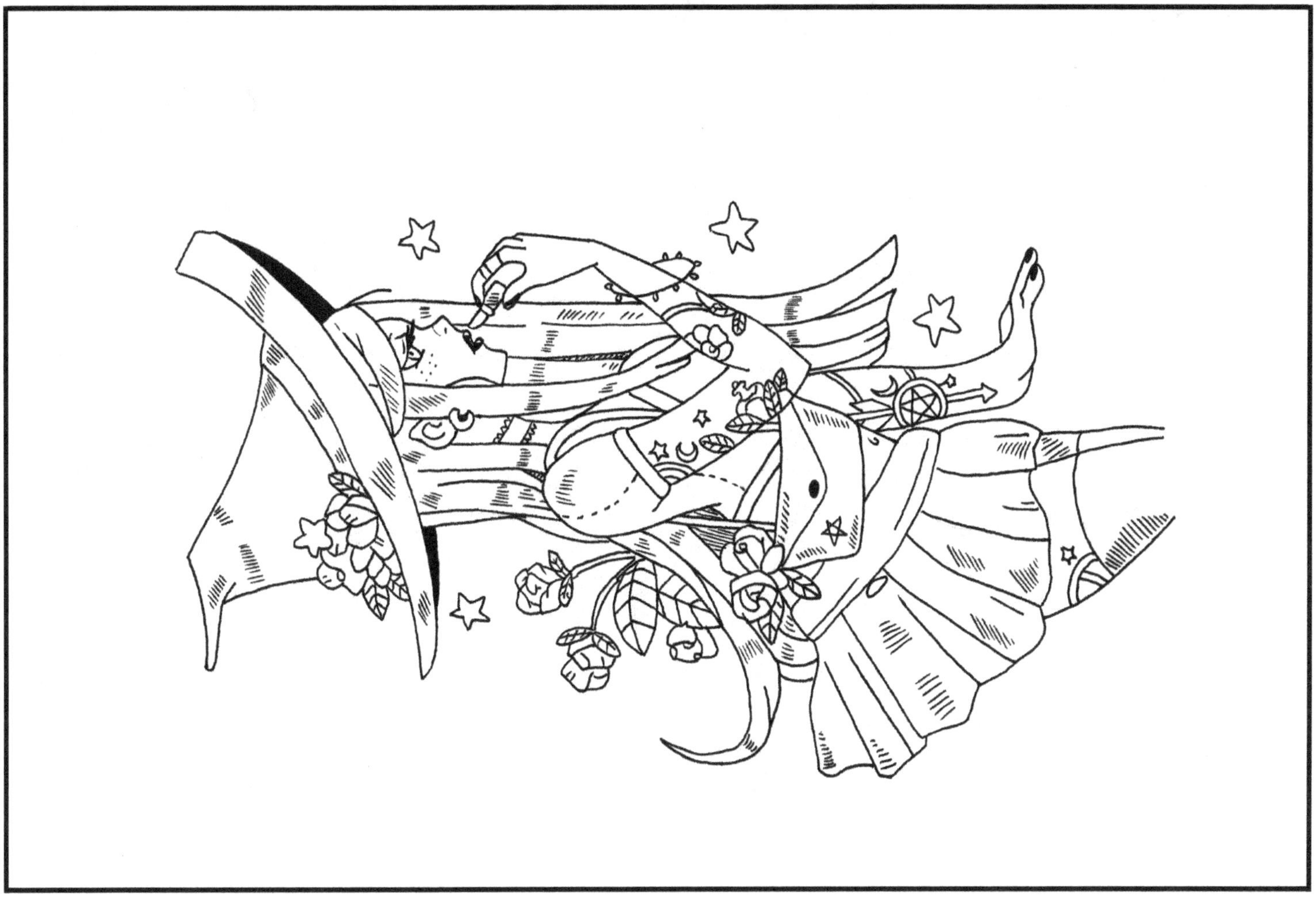

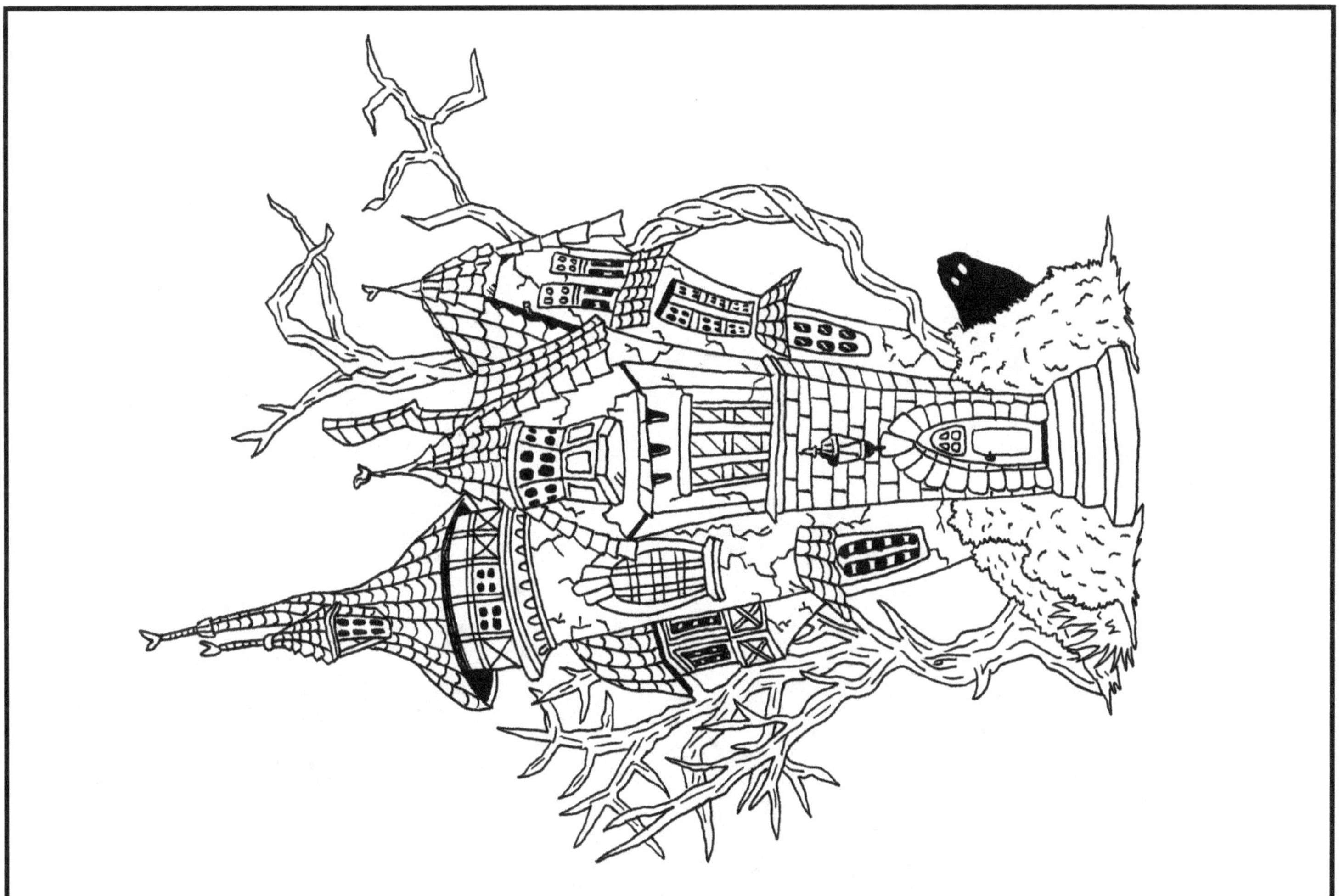

TISKYD Publishing

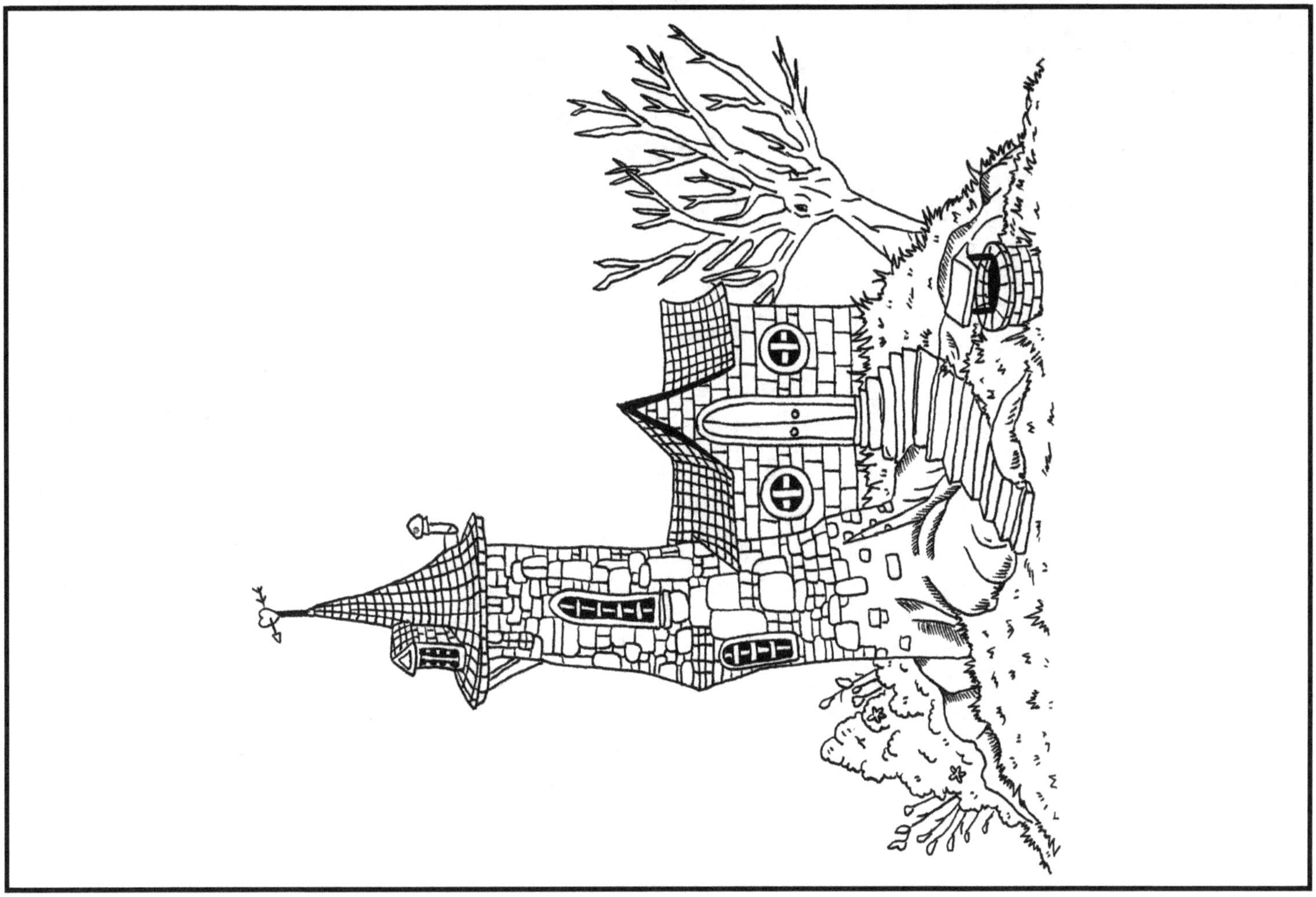

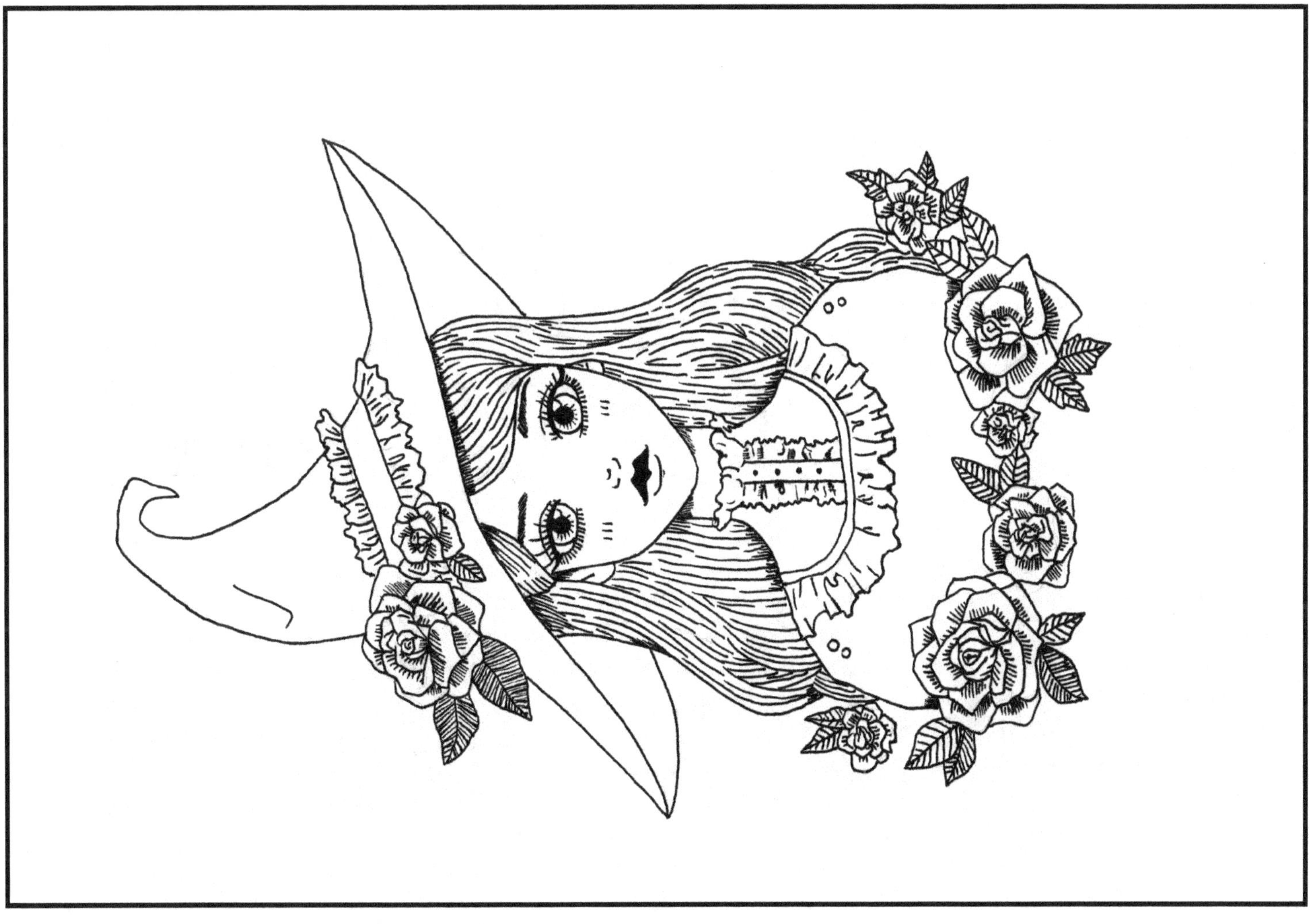

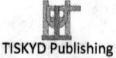

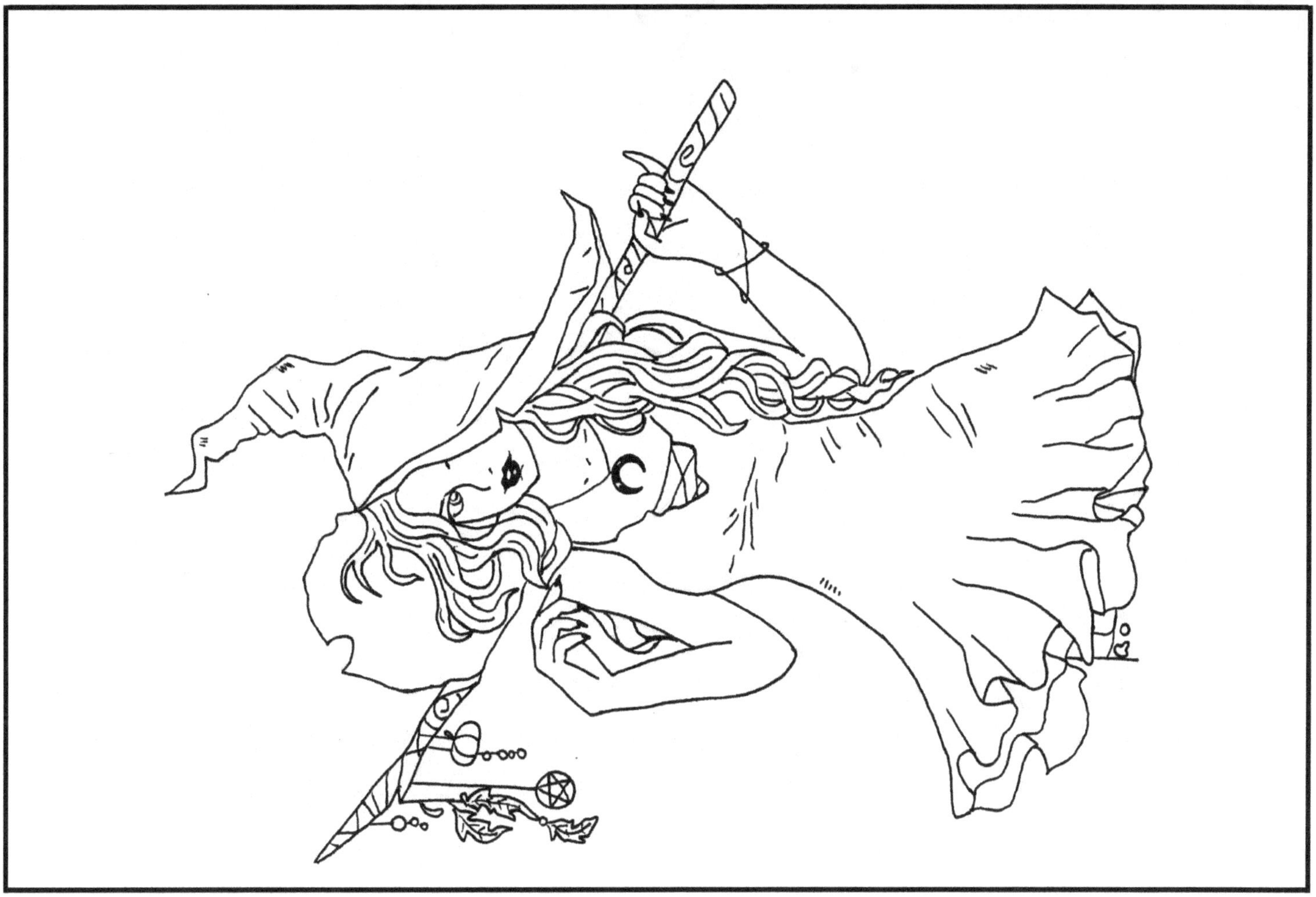

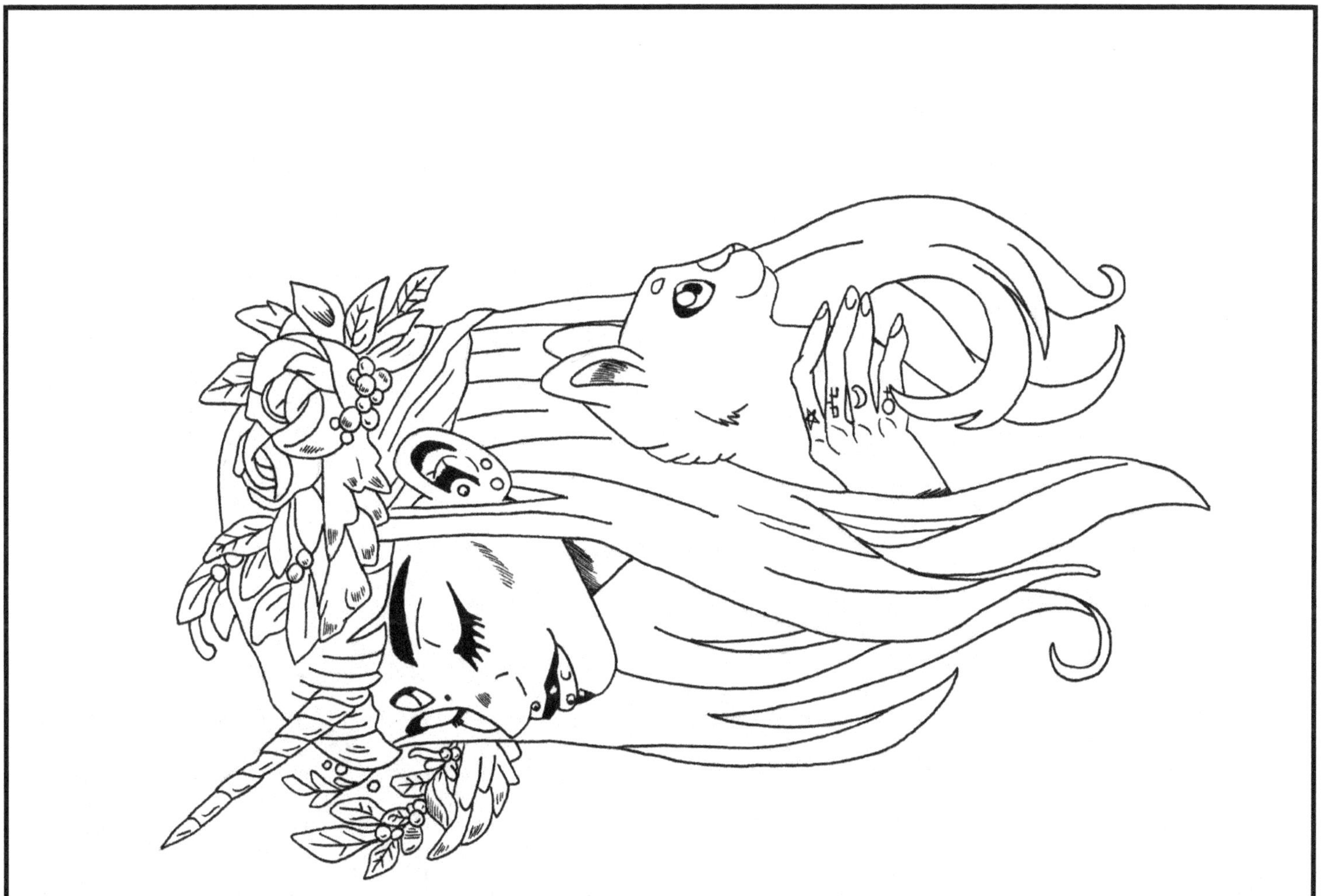

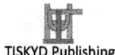

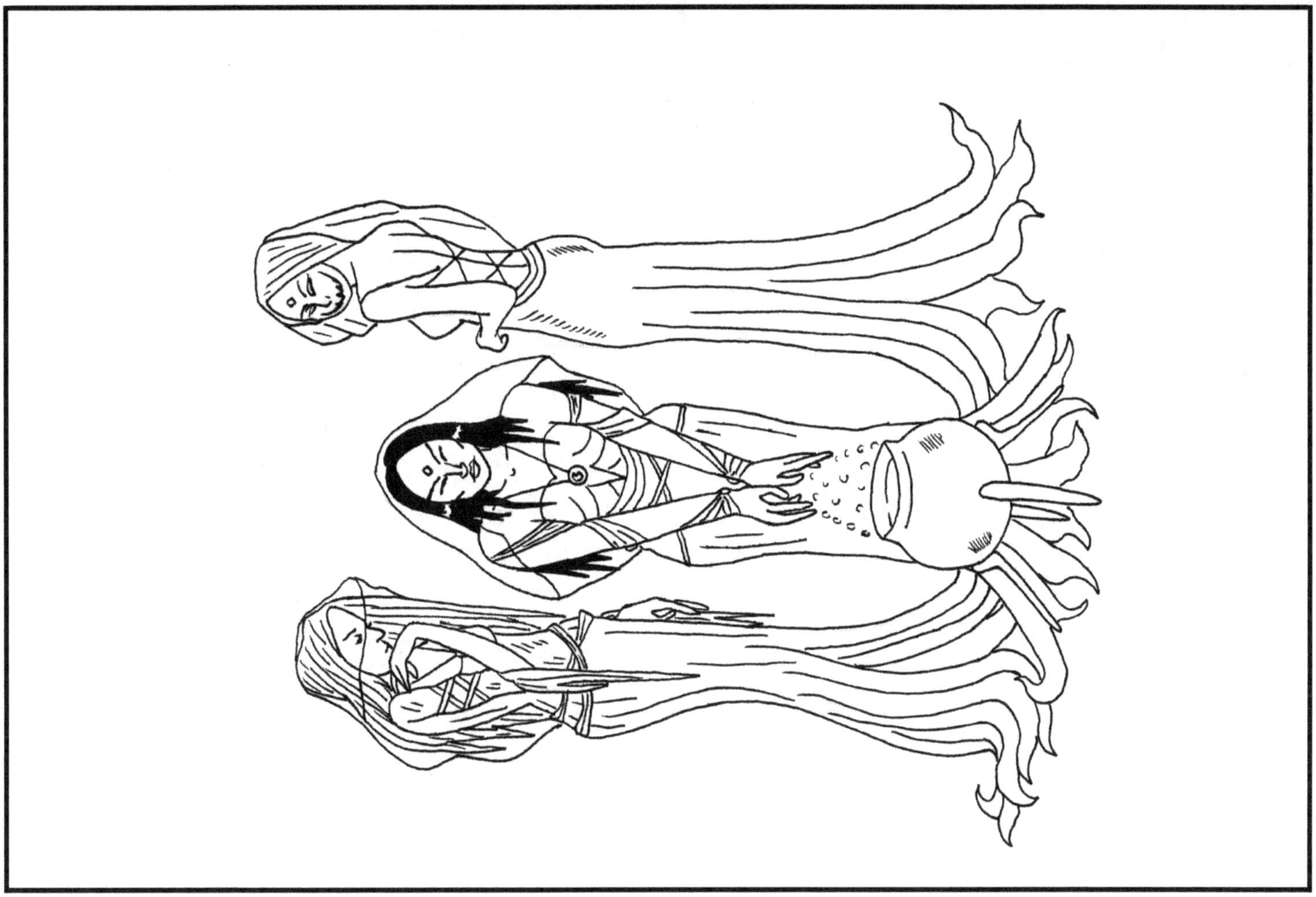

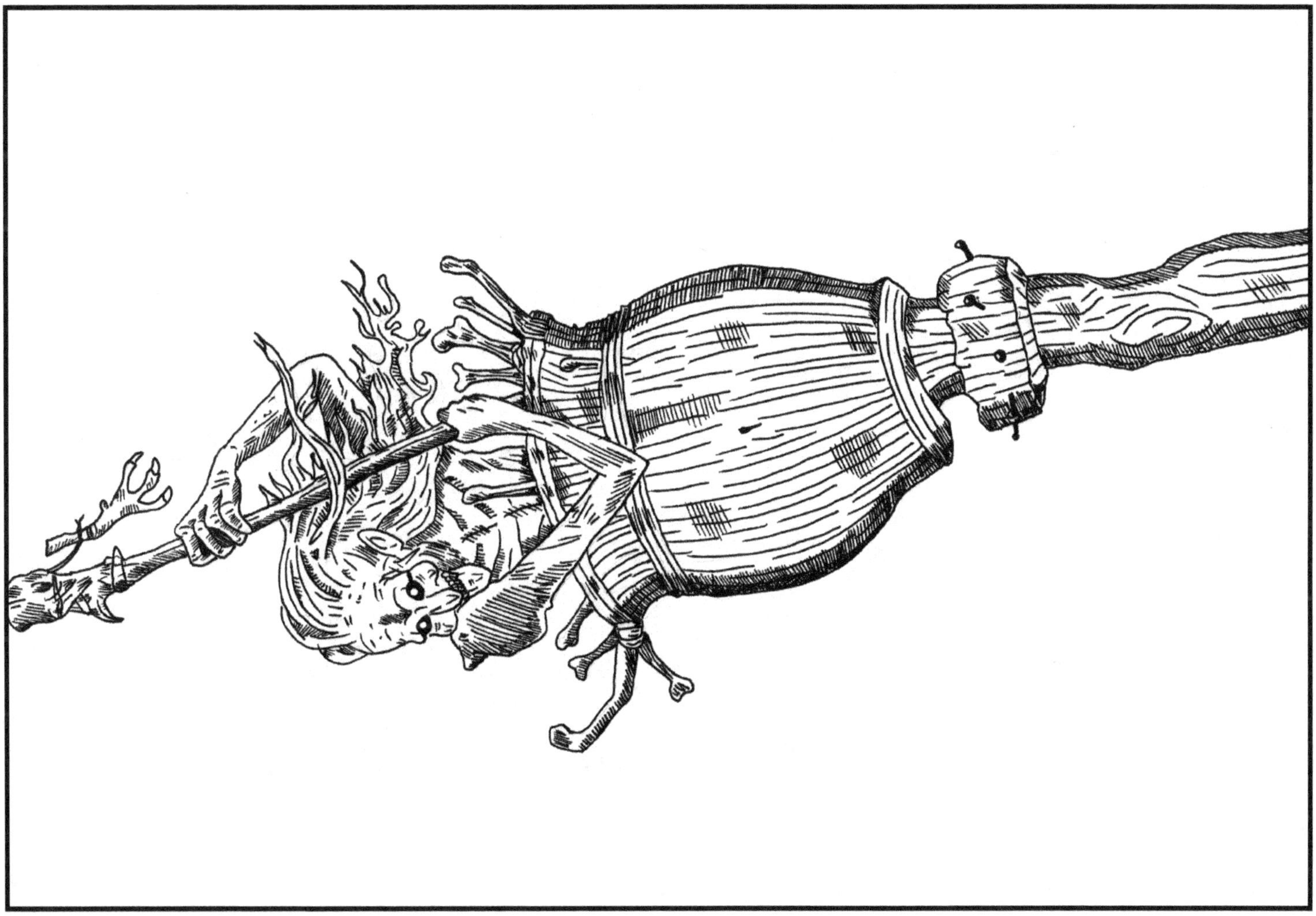

TISKYD Publishing

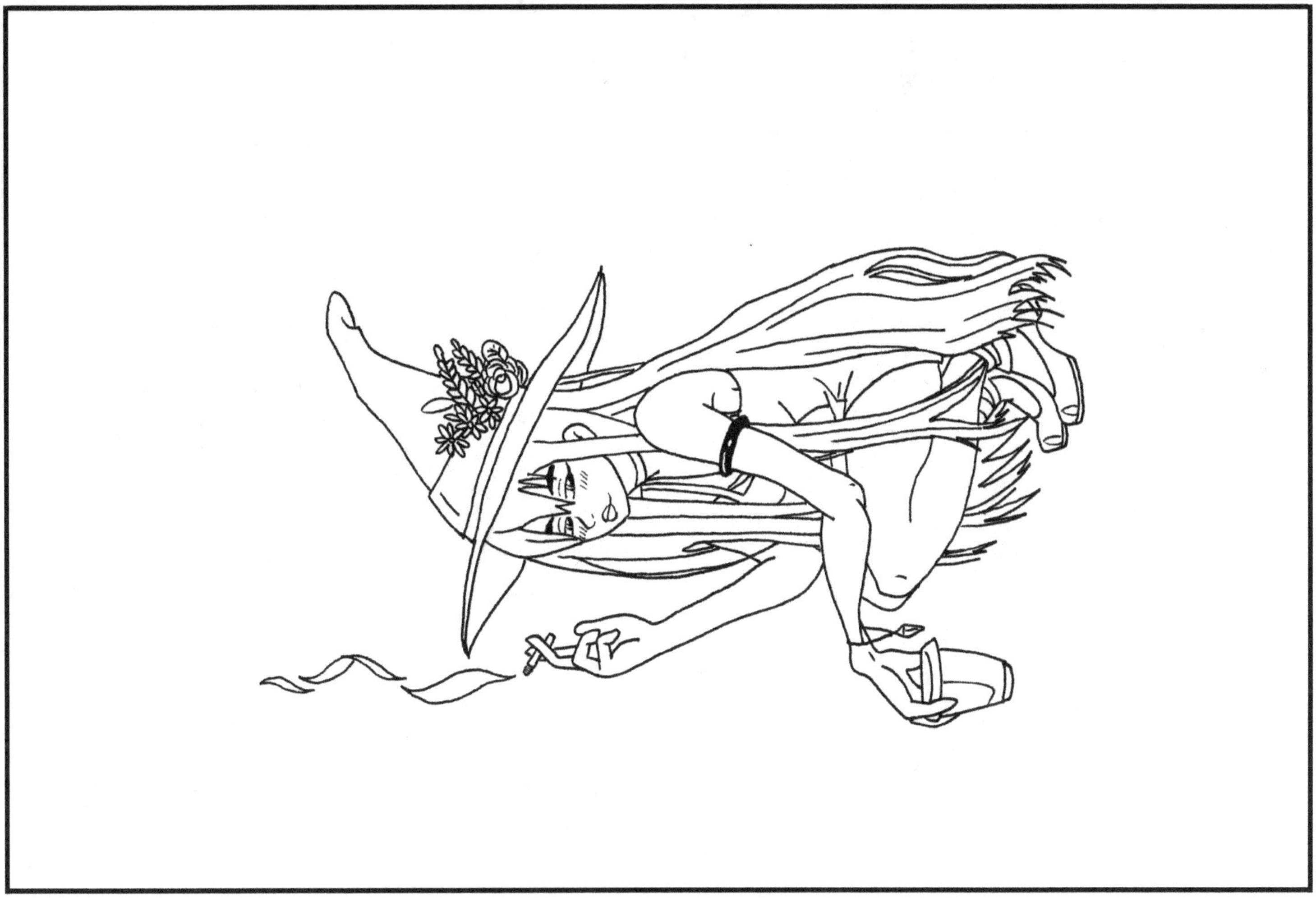

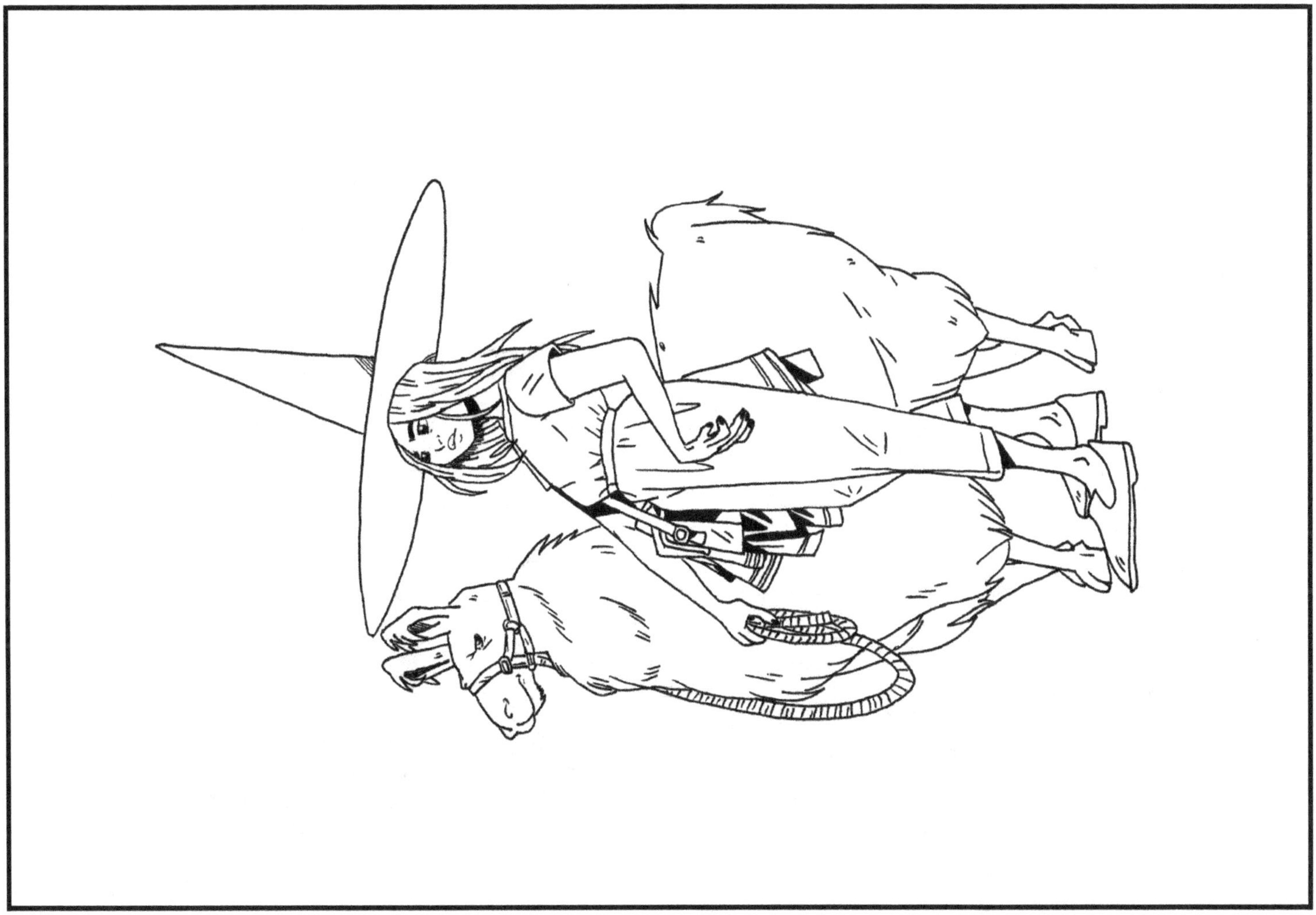

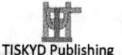

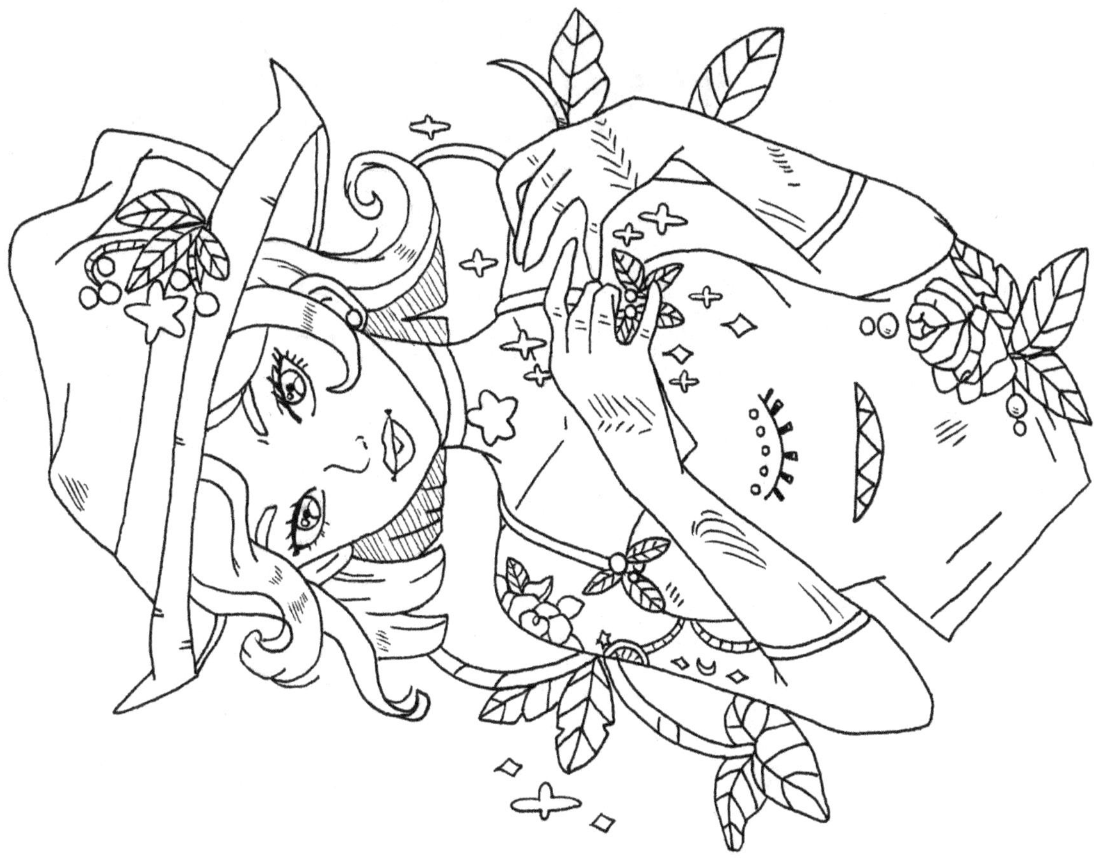

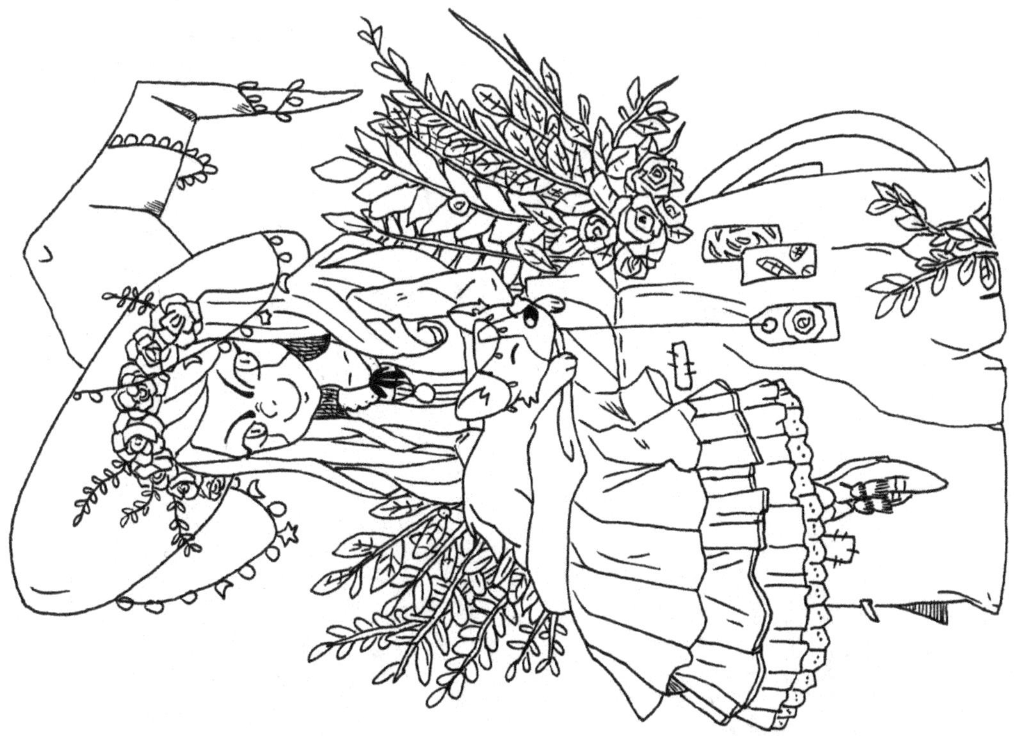

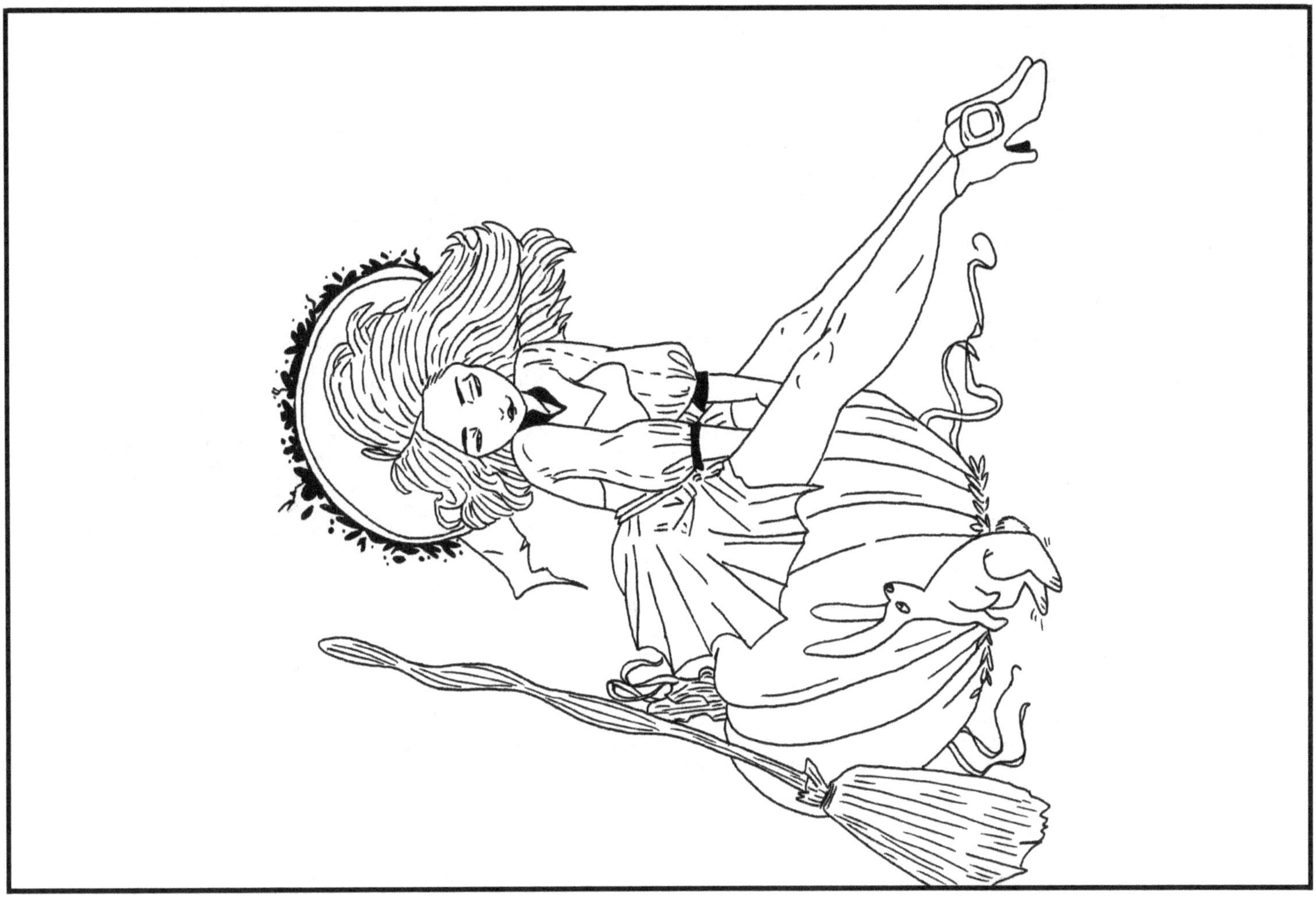

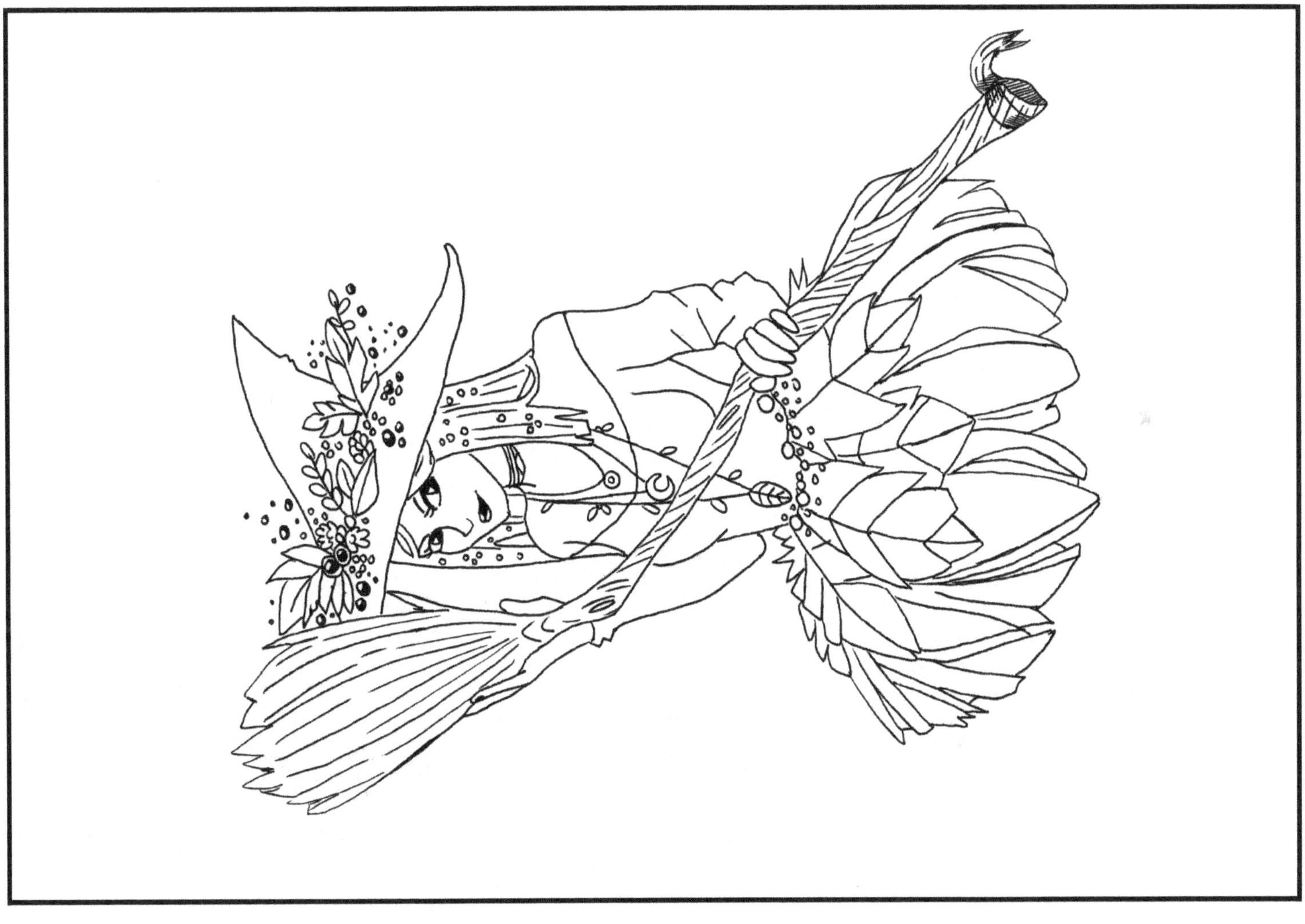

TISKYD Publishing

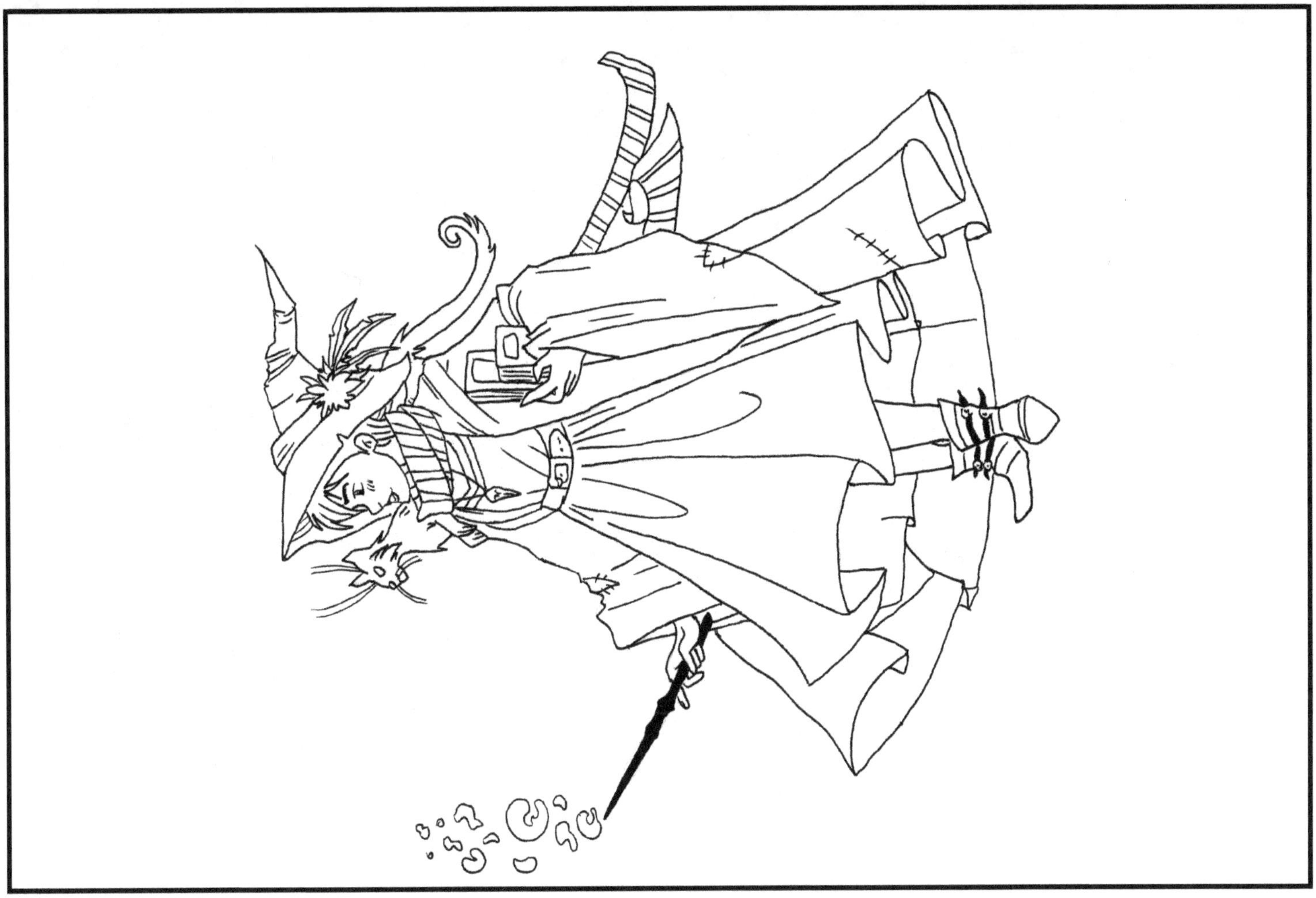

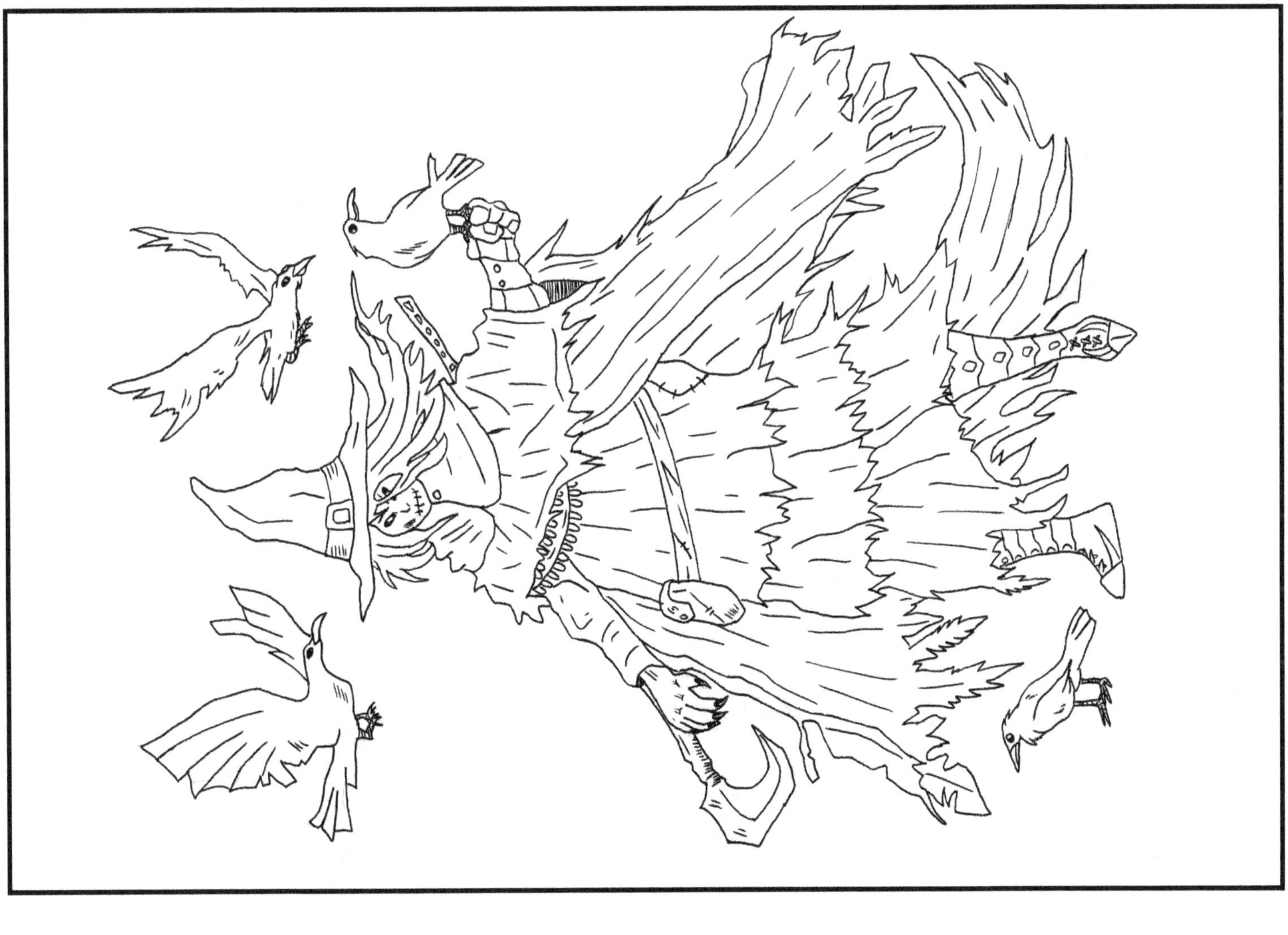

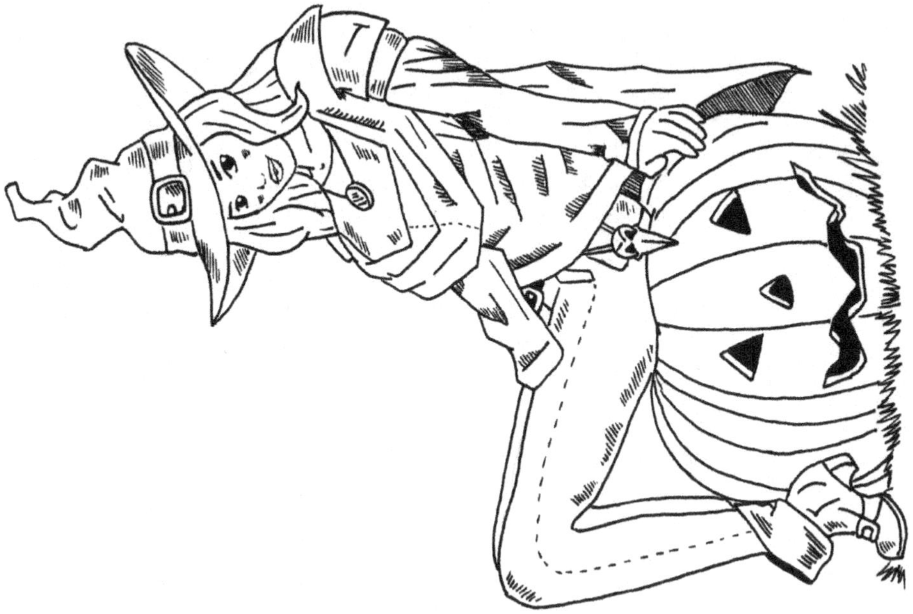

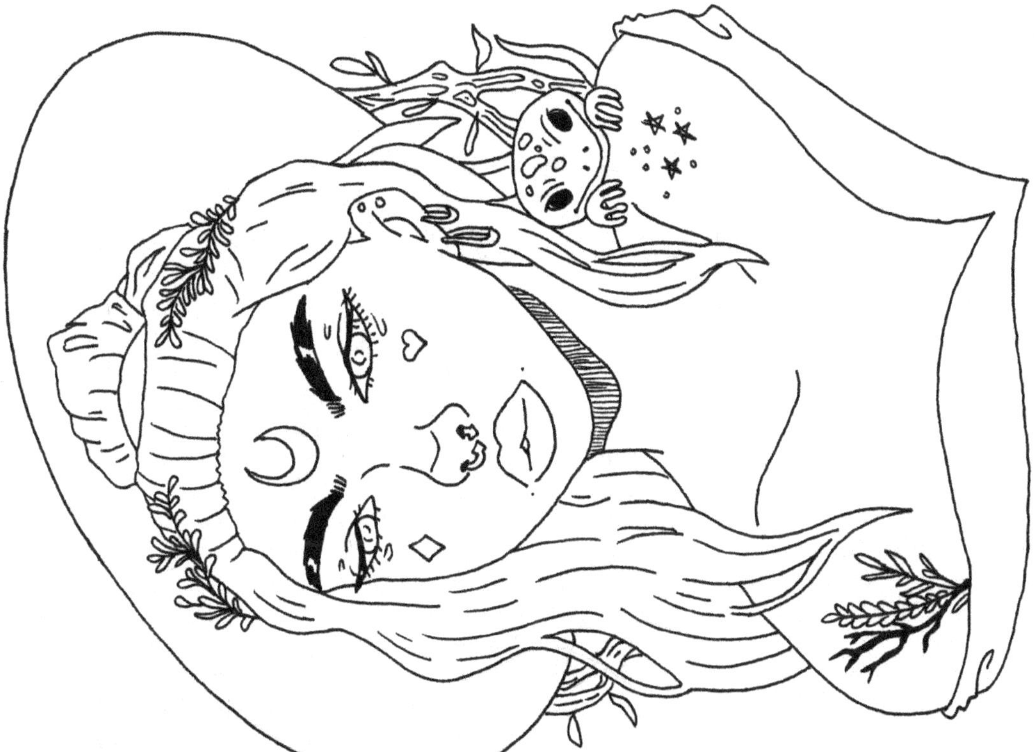

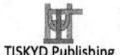

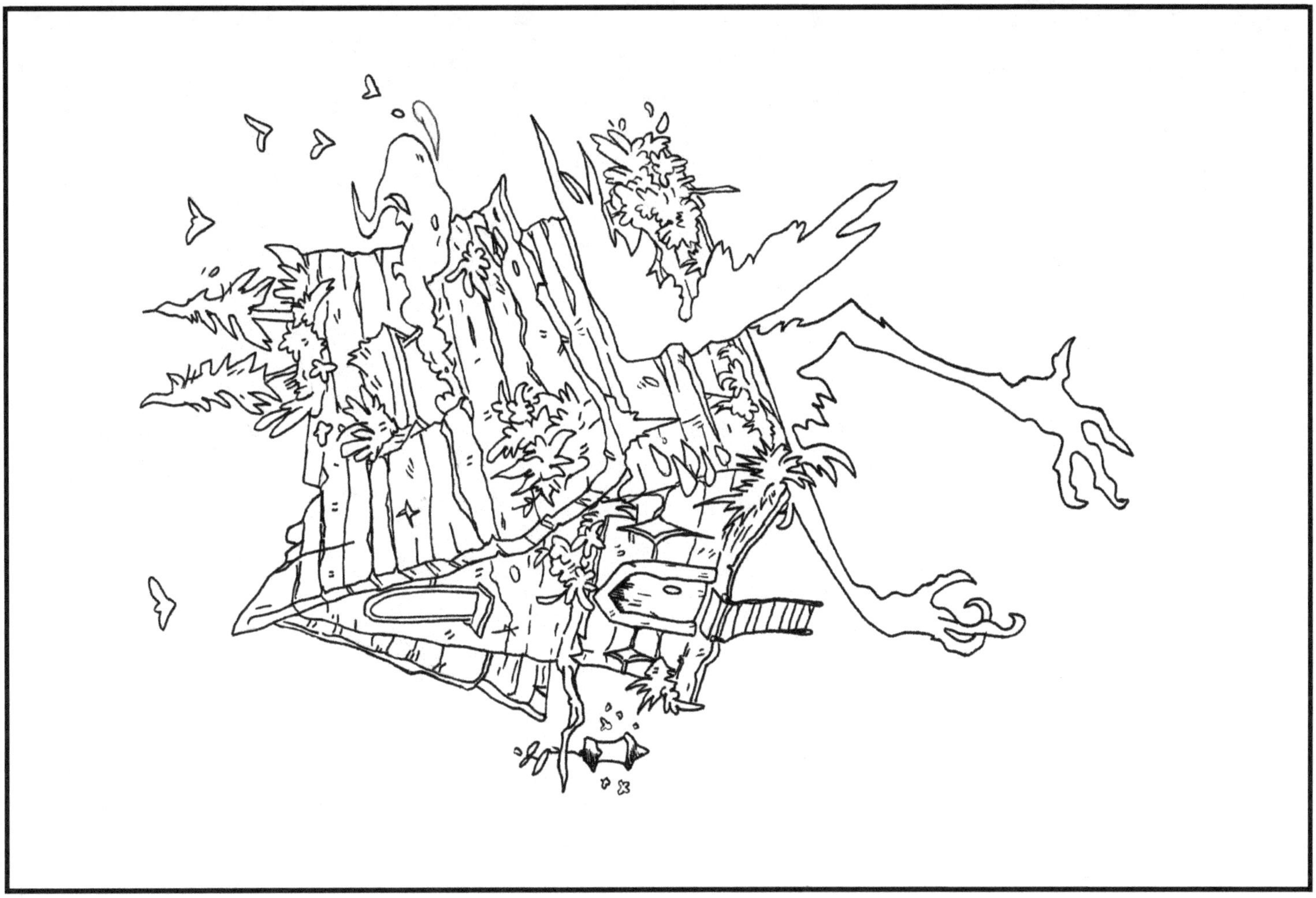

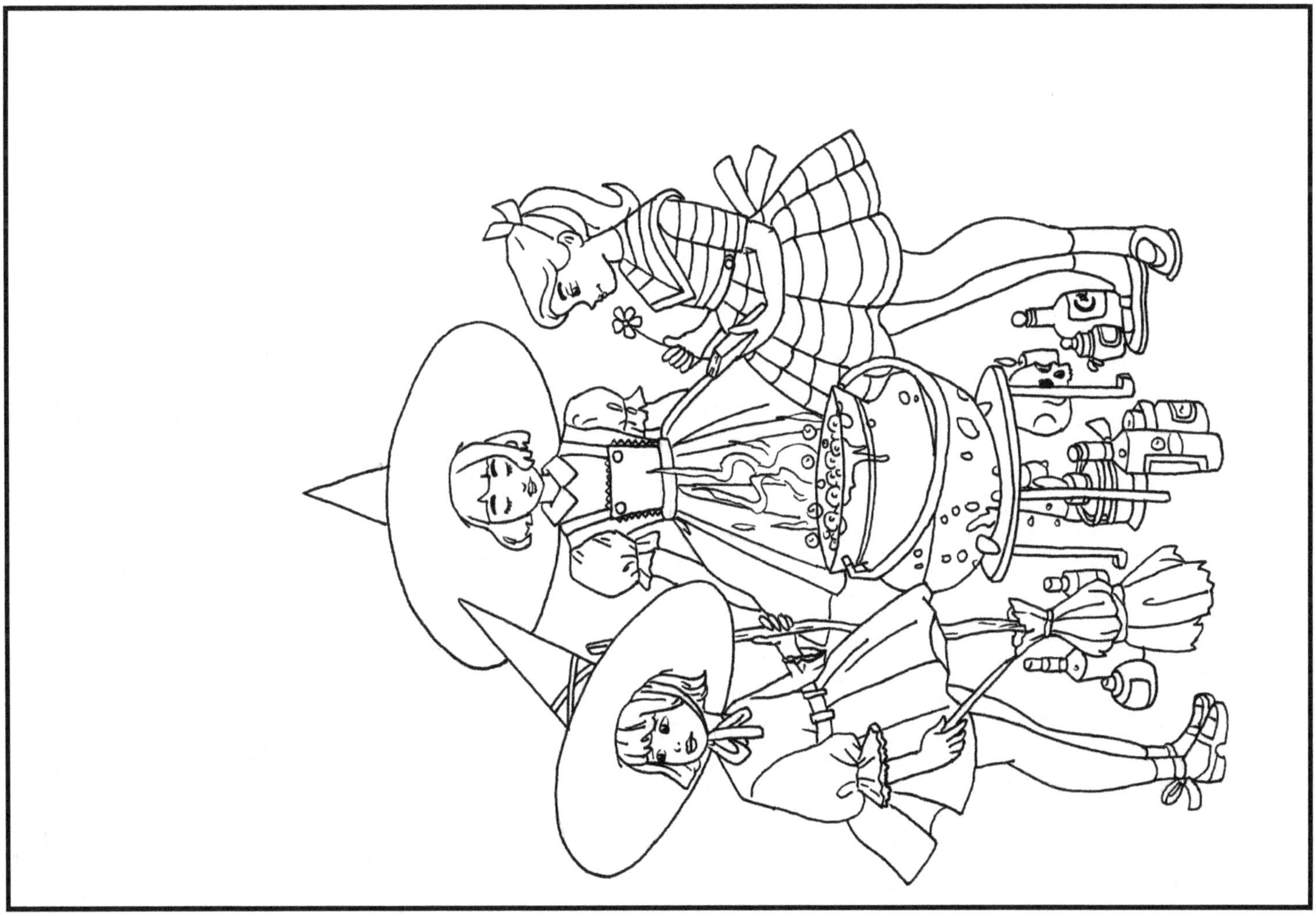

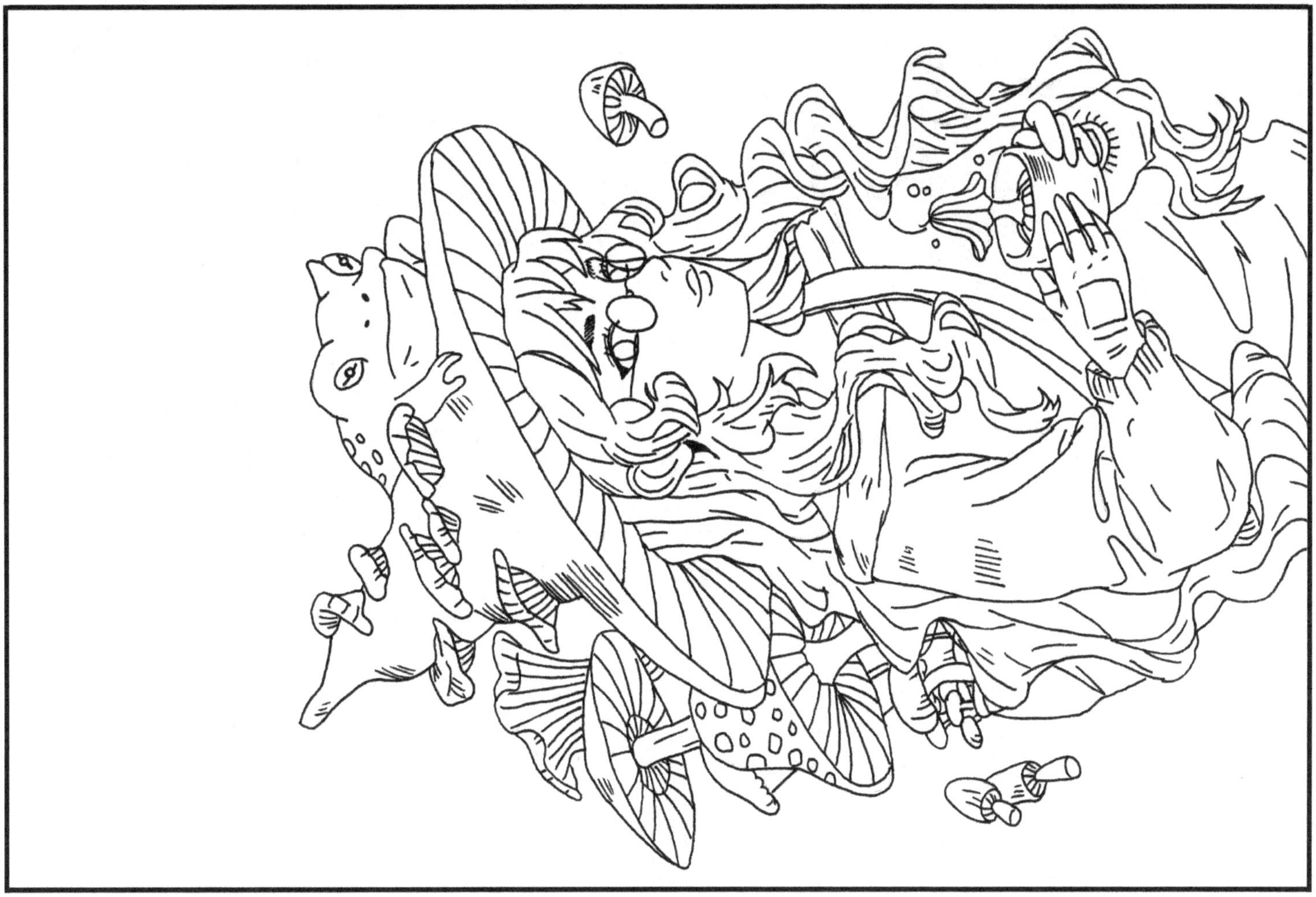

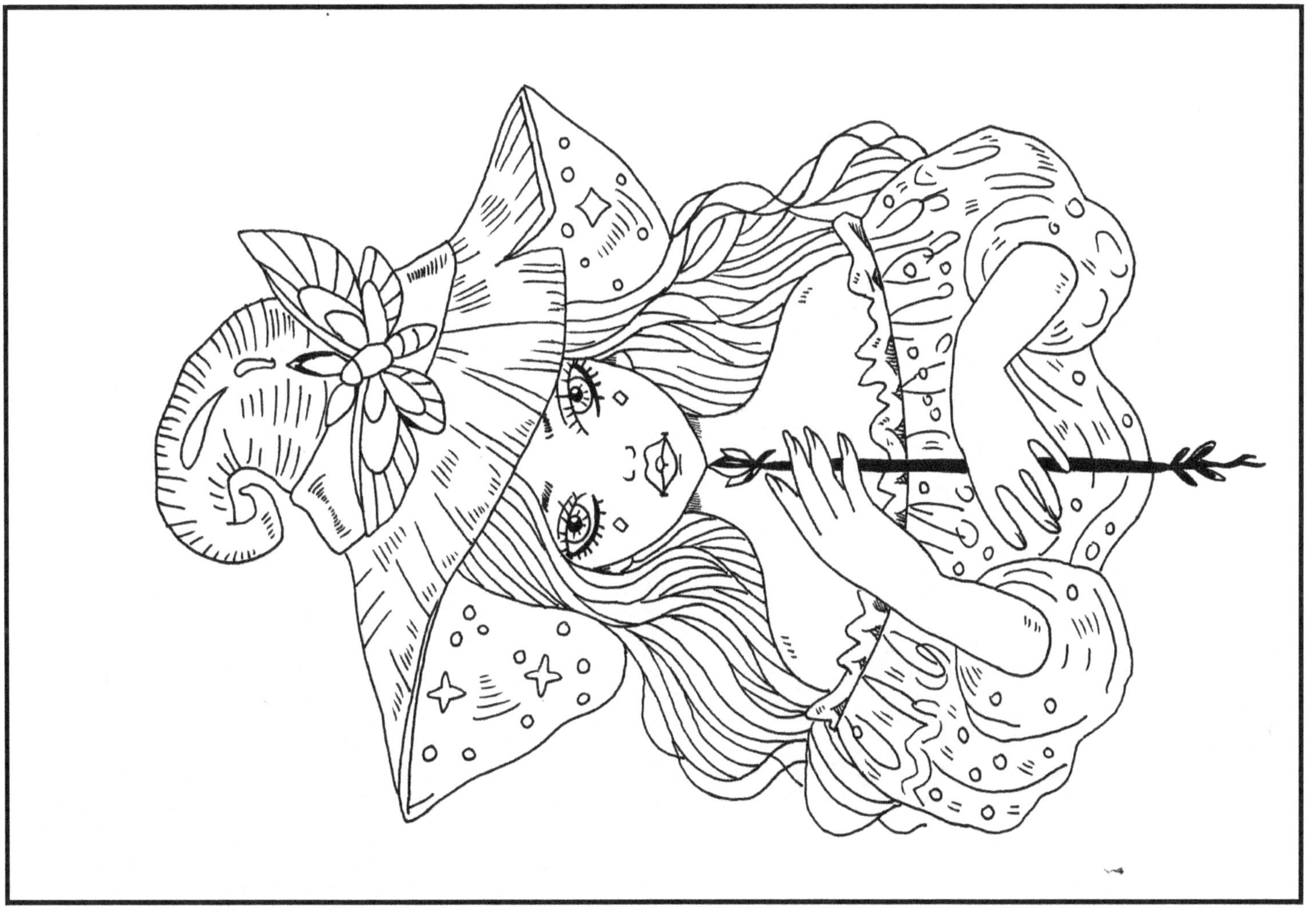

TISKYD Publishing

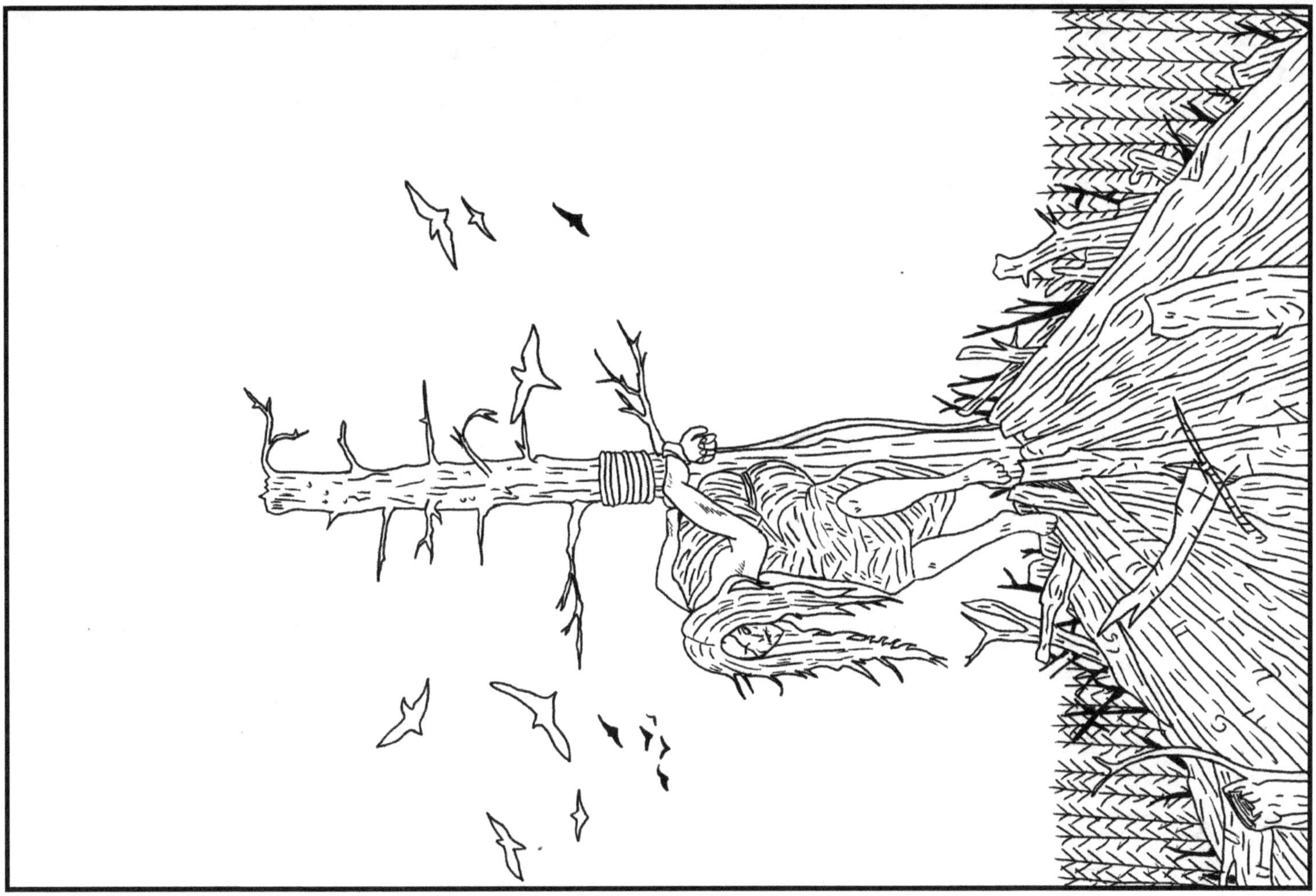

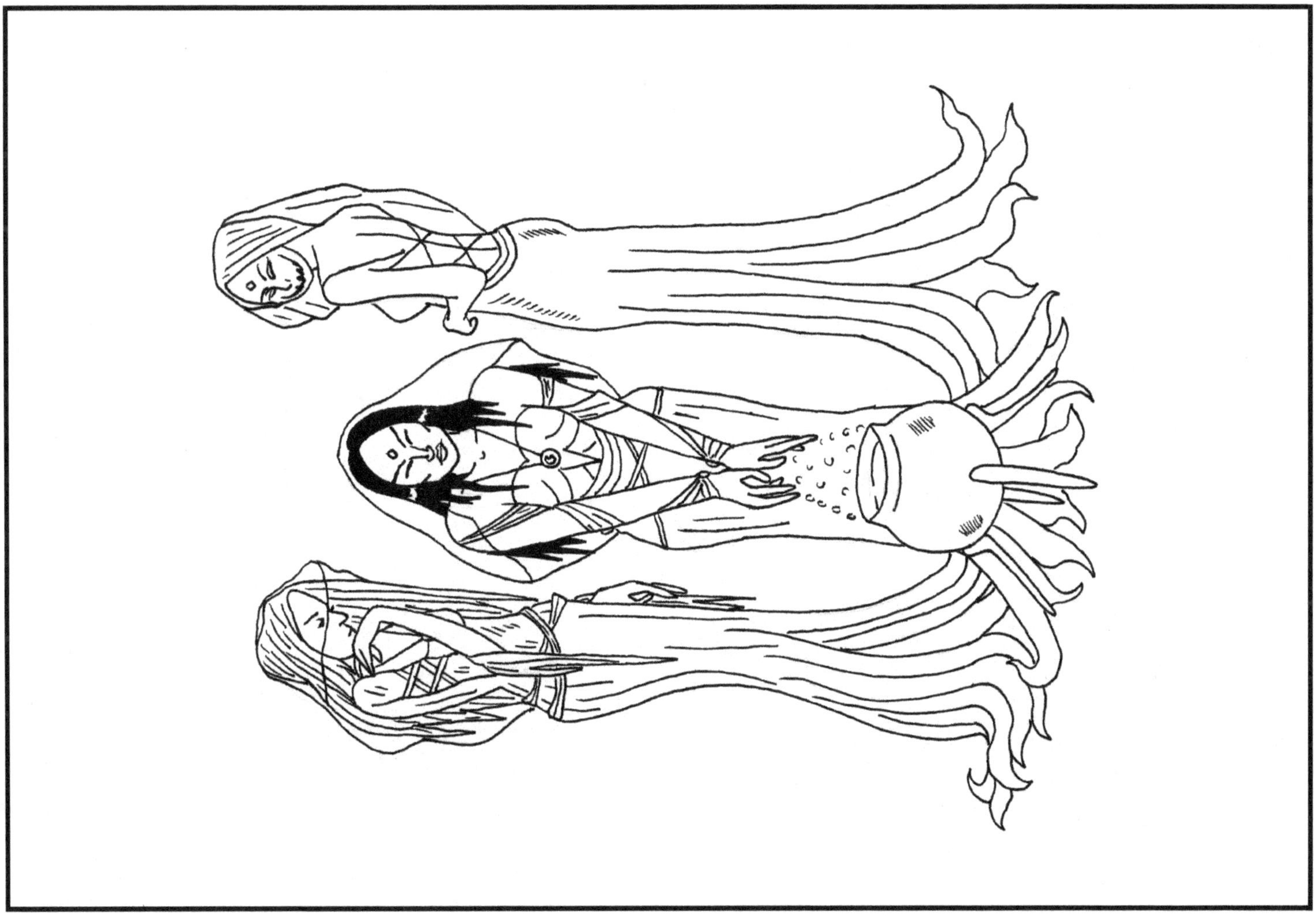

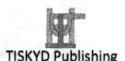

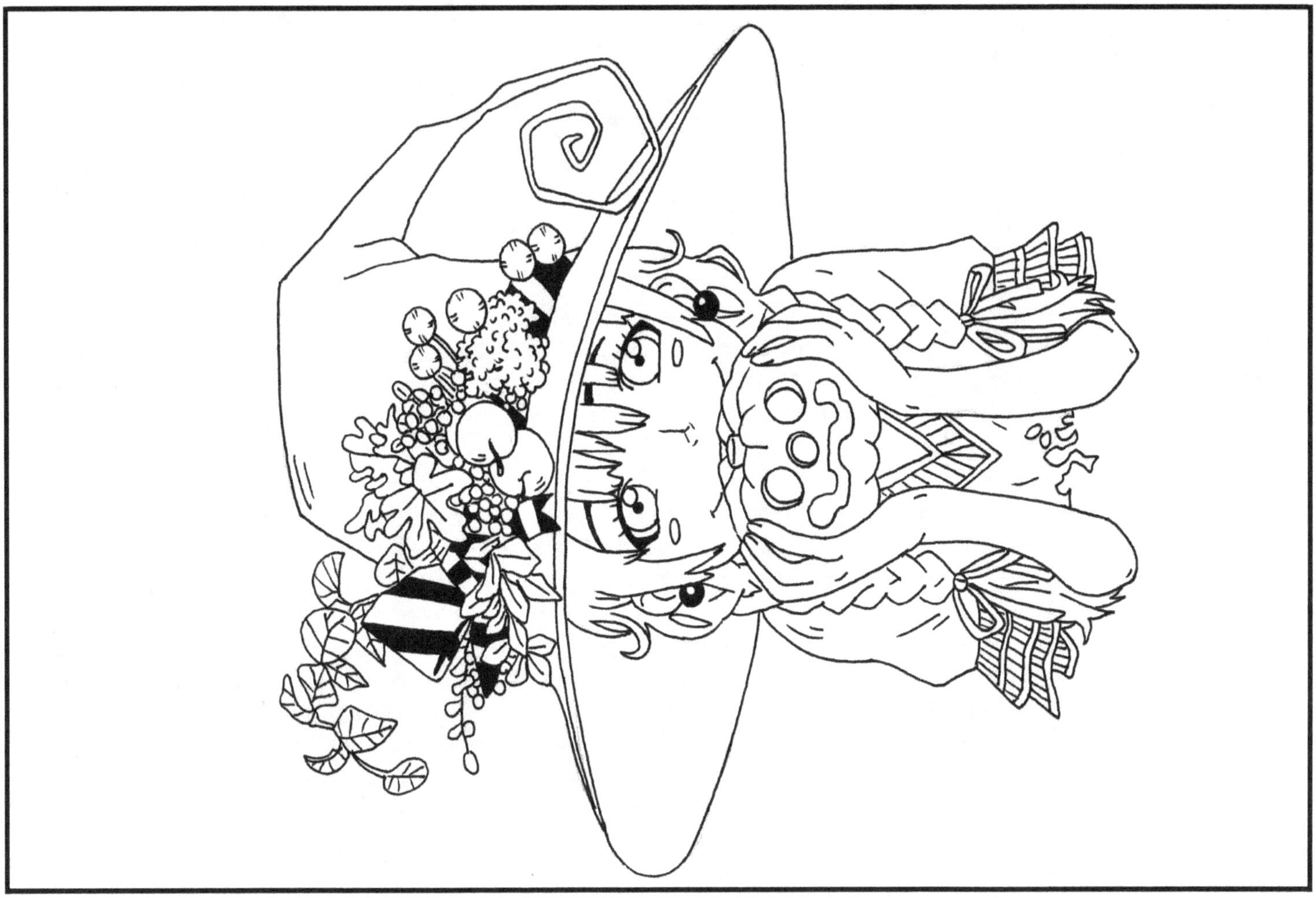

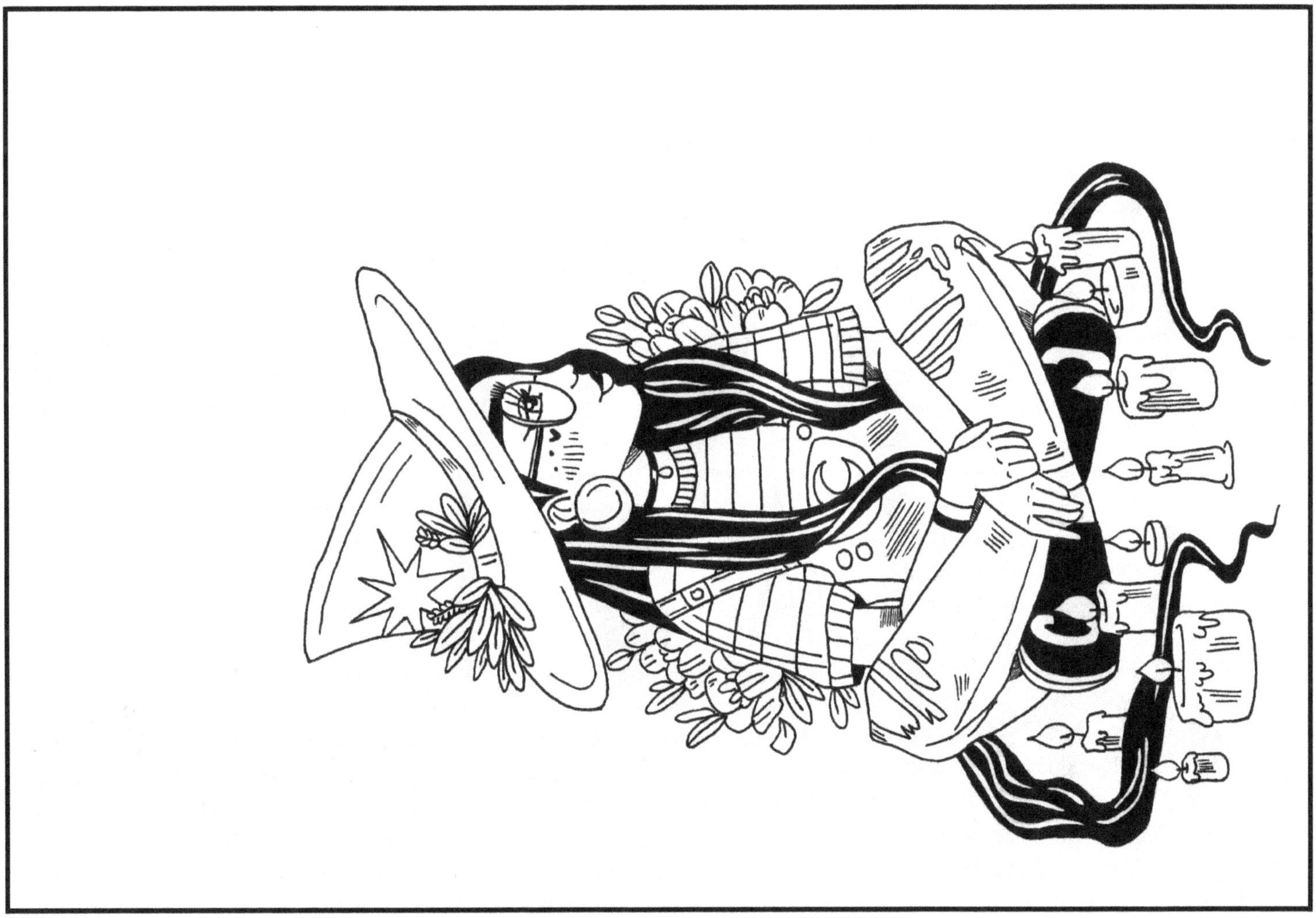

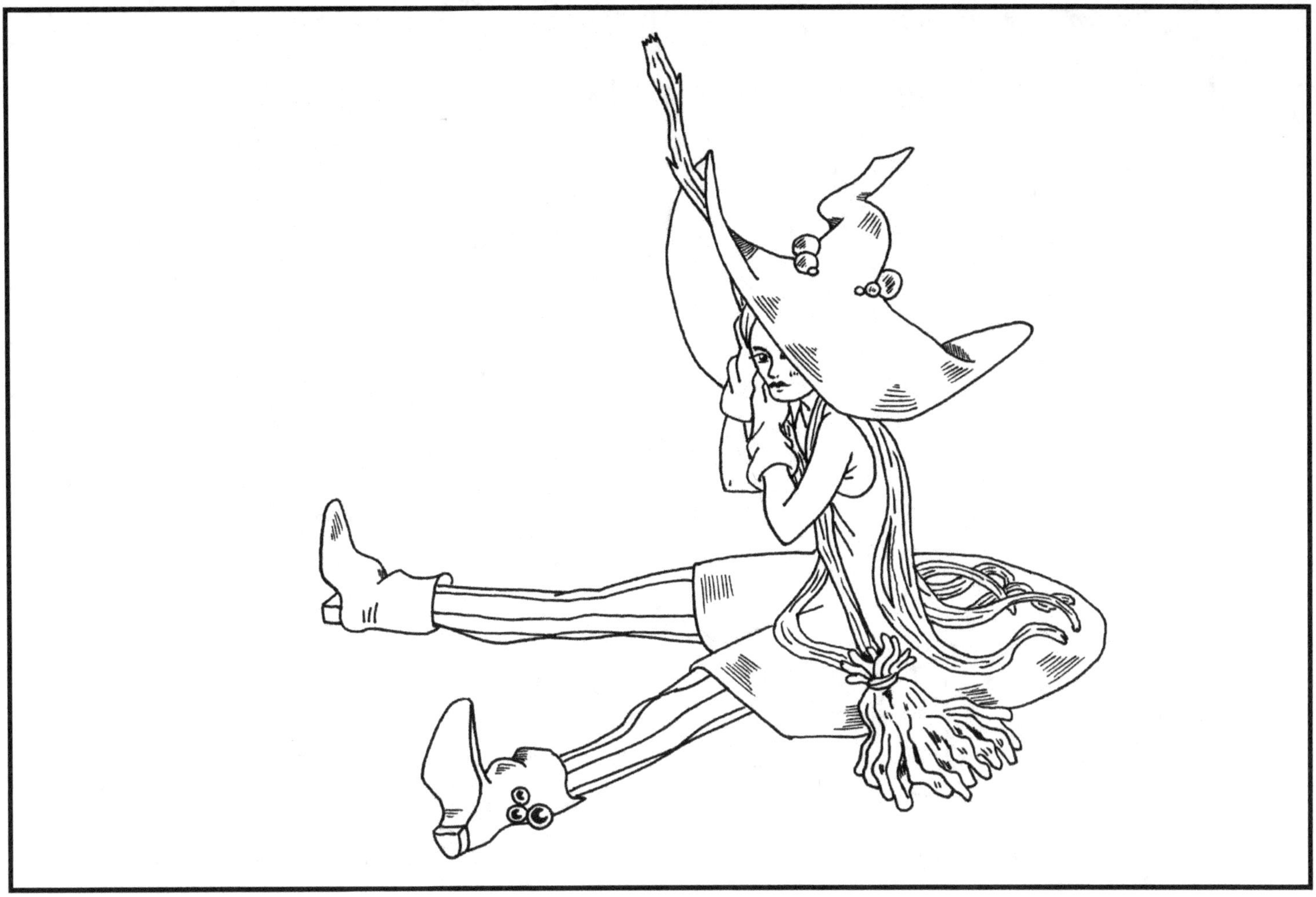

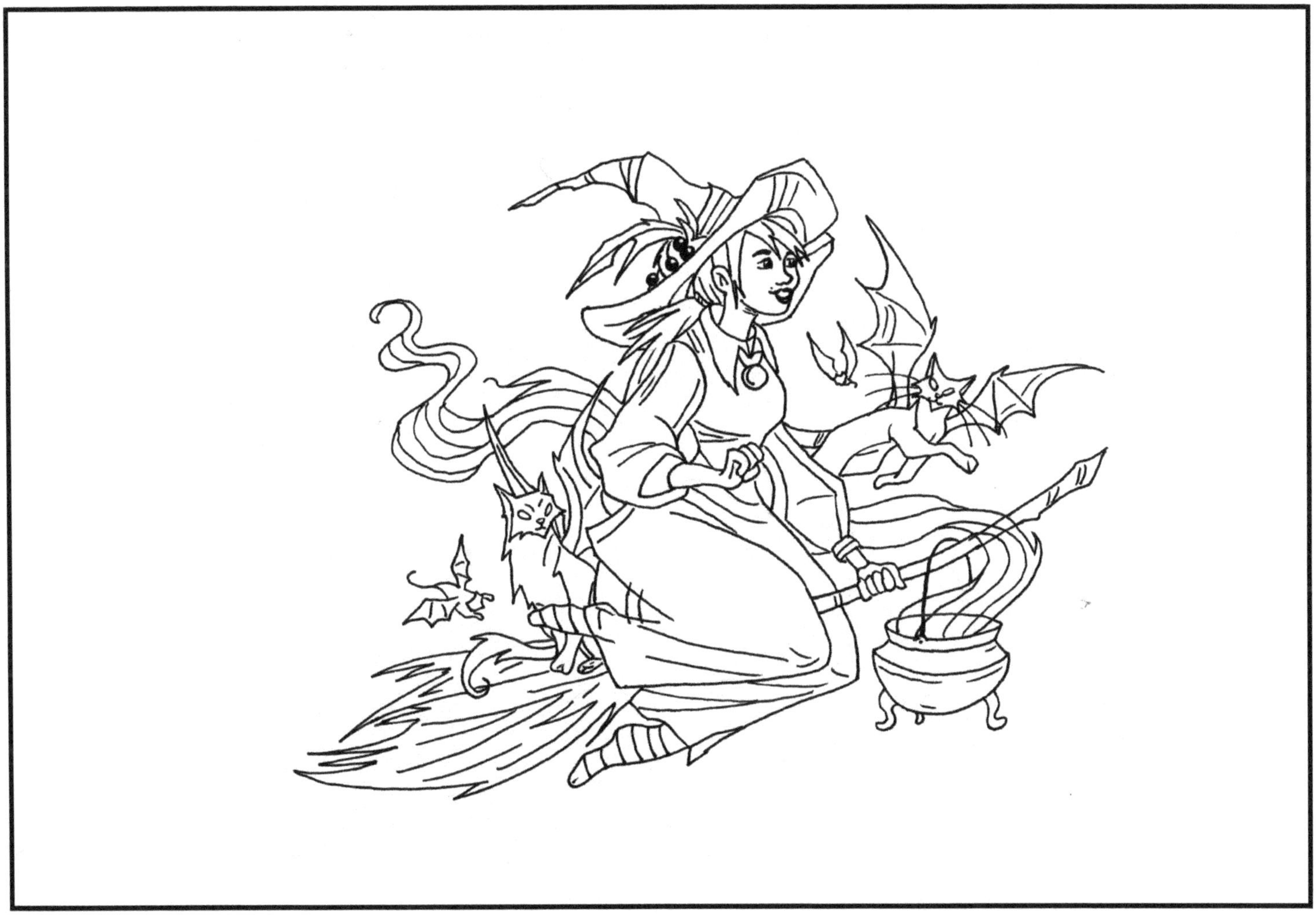

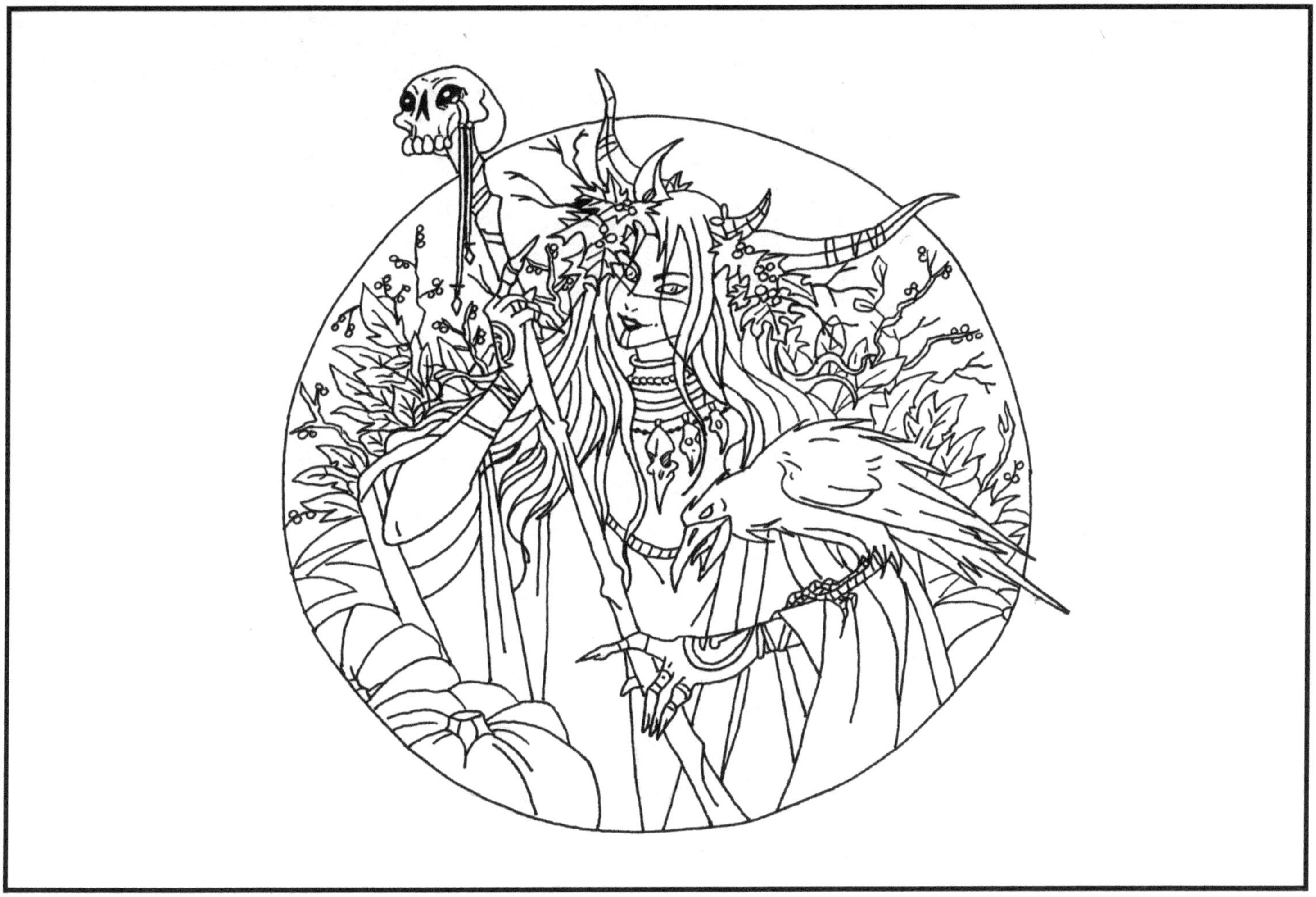

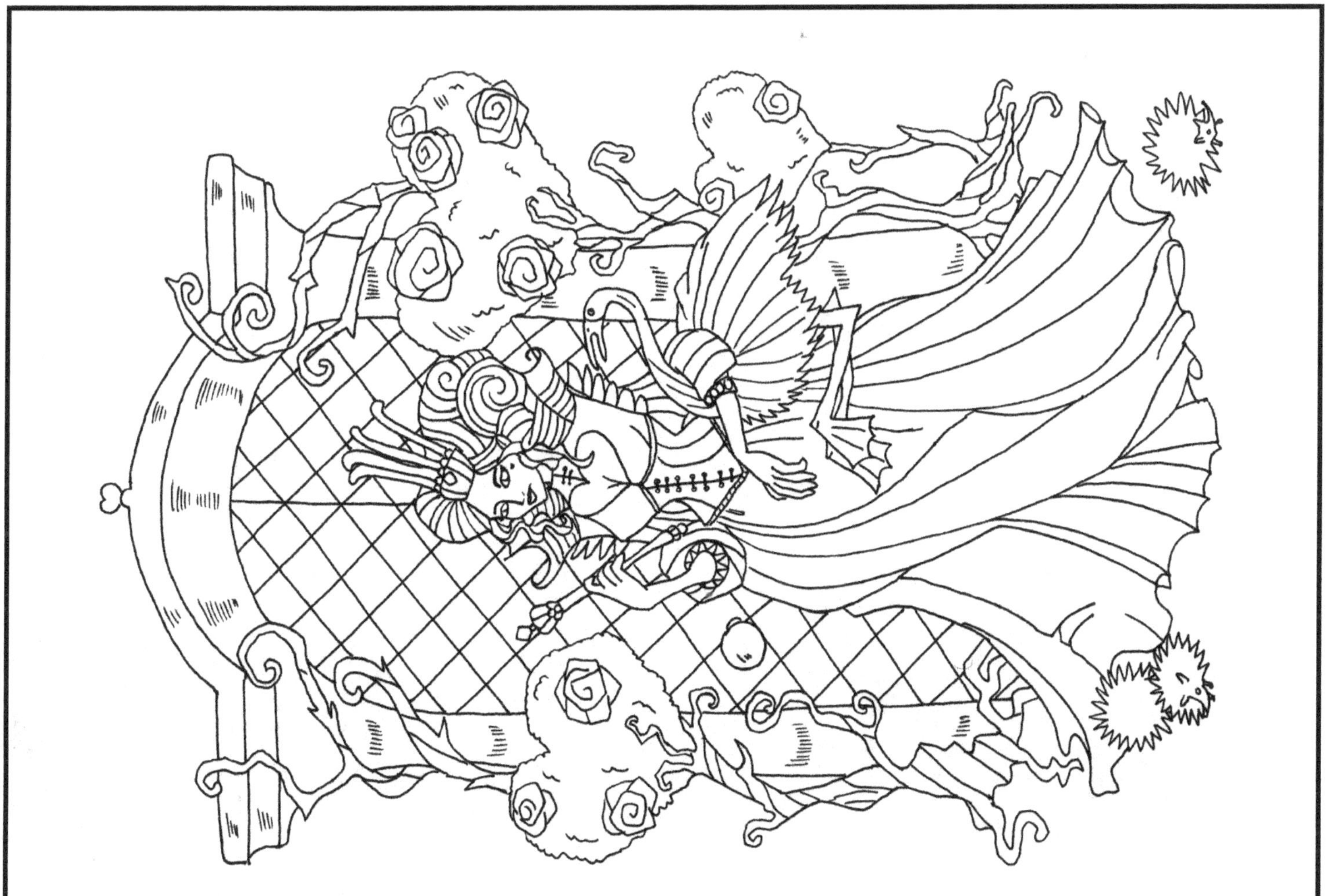

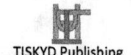

TISKYD Publishing

www.ingramcontent.com/pod-product-compliance
Lightning Source LLC
Chambersburg PA
CBHW080500220526
45465CB00006B/2326